"This book exceeded even my high expectations. I knew Martin and Petro de Lange before they went to Turkey as a young missionary couple, with an earnest desire to share the love of God with the people of that land, willing to give their lives in a foreign country because they were faithful and obedient to the call of God.

"The book is written in such captivating way that I could hardly stop reading it. This real-life story will appeal widely and will undoubtedly touch many lives."

Dr Isak Burger
President of the Apostolic Faith Mission of South Africa

"We urgently need books about Turkey, one of the most unreached nations in the world. Martin and his family have served Jesus in the country of Turkey for thirteen years. This book deserves your attention. Please get extra copies to give to your friends. Use it to mobilize urgently needed prayer and action for Turkey."

George Verwer
Founder of Operation Mobilisation

Belinda Lamprecht grew up in Australia, but felt God's call during university to head to South Africa. Since then, God has led her on an amazing adventure; she has dabbled in children's ministry, taught communities about HIV and AIDS, worked in schools, lived in a township, got married and become the mother of two children.

THE EDGE
OF PARADISE

Turkey is beautiful. But for Christians
there is always a price

Martin de Lange

with Belinda Lamprecht

MONARCH
BOOKS

Oxford, UK & Grand Rapids, Michigan, USA

First published in the UK in 2012 by Monarch Books
(a publishing imprint of Lion Hudson plc)
Wilkinson House, Jordan Hill Road, Oxford OX2 8DR, England
Tel: +44 (0)1865 302750 Fax: +44 (0)1865 302757
Email: monarch@lionhudson.com
www.lionhudson.com

Published in association with DrawBridge Productions, P.O.Box 12391, Mill Street, Cape Town, RSA, 8001
Film Producer/Publishing Agent: Craig Galbraith (email: drawbridgecapetown2@gmail.com)

ISBN 978 0 85721 230 6 (print)
ISBN 978 0 85721 269 6 (Kindle)
ISBN 978 0 85721 270 2 (epub)
ISBN 978 0 85721 271 9 (PDF)

Distributed by:
UK: Marston Book Services, PO Box 269, Abingdon, Oxon OX14 4YN
USA: Kregel Publications, PO Box 2607, Grand Rapids, Michigan 49501

The text paper used in this book has been made from wood independently certified as having come from sustainable forests.

British Library Cataloguing Data
A catalogue record for this book is available from the British Library.

Printed and bound in the UK by Clays Ltd, St Ives plc.

Contents

Map of Turkey	6
Regional Map of South-East Turkey	7
Dedication	8
Foreword	9
Preface	11
Chapter 1	13
Chapter 2	22
Chapter 3	42
Chapter 4	62
Chapter 5	84
Chapter 6	101
Chapter 7	127
Chapter 8	146
Chapter 9	164
Chapter 10	178
Epilogue	187
Your Part in World Missions	189

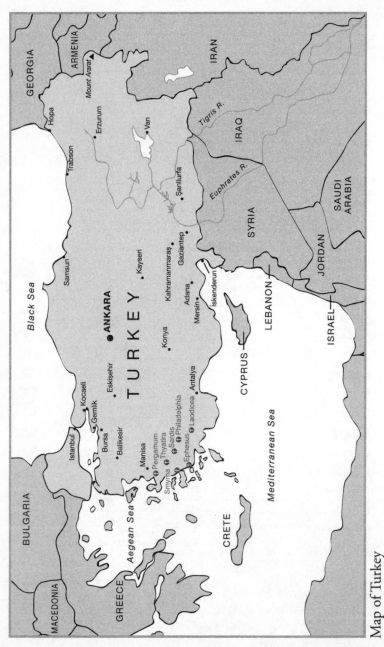

Map of Turkey

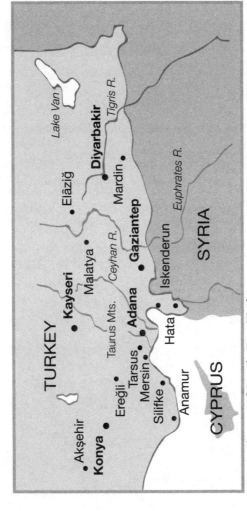

Regional map of South-East Turkey

Thank you
Petro and the boys for your love,
patience and support.
Belinda for putting all my notes into
a gripping, flowing story.
OM South Africa for releasing me
from ministry to finish the writing.

Foreword

During October 2010, 4,200 Christian leaders from 198 countries around the globe gathered in Cape Town, South Africa, for the third Lausanne Congress on world evangelization. As the leaders listened to God and one another, they celebrated what the Lord was doing in the world and spent time to reflect on what the critical challenges for the church in the twenty-first century were. These leaders all agreed that one of the major priorities for the global church was that of discipleship.

The Edge of Paradise, detailing the experiences of Martin and Petro de Lange, is the story of lives lived in radical discipleship. It is a story told in raw honesty, mixed with humility. Not many leaders are willing to make themselves vulnerable by revealing personal feelings and experiences, but in this book Martin does just that. He shows us how to live a life of faith and courage, yet at the same time he is acutely aware of his own human shortcomings. I was impressed by his honesty in describing not only successes, but also disappointments and even failures. Throughout he acknowledges and emphasizes the role the grace of God played in his life. Ordinary people like me can relate to this, and are inspired by lives lived well for God.

I remember well how absolutely grief-stricken Martin and Petro were when they heard of the murder of their friends and colleagues in Turkey. This showed me the deep level of love and care they had for the people to whom they committed their lives.

I have known the de Langes for seventeen years and have seen them live the story told in this book. I believe their example is one to be emulated by the church in Africa and around the world. The book will be an inspiration to those of both this and the next generation who wish to dedicate their lives to spreading the gospel. It highlights the wonderful fact that we, on the continent of Africa, have developed from being simply recipients of the gospel to being part of the global mission force carrying it forth.

One of the criticisms often leveled at Africans is that we do not write enough. Here is a book written by one of the sons of Africa, and it is a proud moment for us. This is a book by one who has dared to live on the edge. It is a well-chronicled story, well written and yet easy to read. I believe you will be encouraged and inspired to dare to dream with God.

Enjoy the read and then share the story with others!

Peter Tarantal
Chairman: Wensa (World Evangelization Network of South Africa);
Southern Africa Director: Mani (Movement for African National Initiatives)

Preface

The eastern part of Turkey is a dry and arid land. Between towering, craggy mountains, strong rivers are born, beginning their journey down to the south of Turkey and then on, into Iraq. This area was historically a part of Mesopotamia, a region mentioned several times throughout the Bible and famously bordered by two mighty watercourses, the Tigris to the west and the Euphrates to the east. The same two rivers are traditionally recognized to have formed part of the boundaries to a far more ancient place, the Garden of Eden – Paradise.

For a number of years, my young family and I lived just fifty kilometers to the west of the Euphrates River, in the city of Malatya. Geographically, it was as though we were living right on the edge of Paradise. The momentous significance of the region would often strike me anew as I crossed this river, going about my work of planting churches and distributing the Bible in some of the very areas where both church and Bible had been born, ages before.

The reality of the danger in which we lived to carry out this work was never far from my mind. Not receiving a fixed income, we trusted God to provide all our needs. At a time when negative attitudes towards Christians, and particularly Christian workers, prevailed and were fostered by the government, we never knew what harm might befall us. We worked in faith, facing every day the real threat of suffering, persecution and death. We lived never knowing when we might be called upon to take the final step across the boundary of our earthly lives into eternity.

We lived on the edge of Paradise.

This book has been written as a tribute to three of my co-workers and best friends: Tilmann Geske, Necati Aydin, and Uğur Yüksel, who paid the highest price for their faith in the Lord Jesus, as they labored faithfully for Him. They entered Paradise, giving their lives for what they believed in and as a sacrifice to Him whom they loved. With this book, I want to honor them, as well as those they left behind.

Chapter 1

The poor guy beside me was already turning green, and the autopsy had hardly even begun.

I was nervous myself, but there was too much riding on this for me to lose my cool. Despite all the training and preparations my buddy next to me and I had been through together, our initiation into the Special Crime Scene Investigation Unit of the South African police force would not be complete without successfully passing this, our first ever post-mortem examination. There had been all kinds of pressure and ribbing from our senior officers the preceding week. They had made some scathing predictions about who would last the longest, and which of us would make a hasty trip to the bathroom to lose our breakfast. However, that morning I arrived at the Pretoria Provincial Hospital morgue with the same hard-headed determination to prove people wrong with which I usually faced life.

My colleague groaned softly and hurriedly stumbled back towards the gauze-covered swing doors as, with the dull whine of an electrical saw, the professor began to open up the skull of the big body lying on the steel table.

"One down," the professor muttered into his cloth mask,

with a quick glance at my retreating friend, "one to go."

I was not going anywhere. My initial hesitation faded as I watched, with a sense of wonder, how the skilled physician began to expose the thin outer membrane enveloping the brain and spinal cord of the body before cutting into and examining the brain itself. After the chest had been sawn open in the same way, each slippery organ was removed from the body cavity and weighed. There, in the good professor's hands, were the very components that made up my own living, breathing body. I was fascinated.

I had always enjoyed pulling things apart, seeing how they worked, modifying and improving them where possible. One of my earliest memories was of lying underneath my go-kart, tinkering and toying (and swearing, when appropriately frustrated) just like my dad did with his own big car; but here, in this dead man's gaping chest, was a mesmerizing engine far more complex than anything else I had ever witnessed before.

"You still here?" the professor finally asked, wiping his hands on his apron. "You've lasted longer than they usually do. You sure this is your first time?"

It *was* my first time, but it wasn't going to be my last.

I joined the South African Police Force in 1984, when I was just seventeen years old, urged to do so by a couple of friends that I had from way back in primary school. I was not the type of person who was easily persuaded and was more likely to stick to my guns stubbornly in any argument, even when wrong, than comply just to please someone. In this particular situation, however, out of loyalty to my friends and not really knowing what I wanted in life, it didn't seem to be a bad idea to do what they had suggested.

It was a decision which turned out to have been guided by Providence in disguise. I discovered a real passion for police work and the discipline, ingenuity and sometimes recklessness required to succeed appealed to me. Even better – I was actually good at it. My work with the forensic unit was varied and, at least as far as I saw it, always incredibly exciting. When on duty, I would speed, sirens blaring, to the scene of violent crimes – murders, suicides and fatal accidents – where, if I were the first to arrive, I would cordon off the area and take note of any potentially useful evidence. My trusty Ricoh camera went with me everywhere in a large aluminum case with all the necessary accessories. It was usually my responsibility to take photographs of anything that might be of potential interest to the scientists and lawyers who would eventually deal with the case. Footprints, broken glass, hair and blood sprays were all captured on film through my wide-angle lens.

Over time, I became quite intuitive about knowing what to look for and learnt to spot the tell-tale signs of foul play. I recall one occasion when I was called to the scene of what had been reported as a fatal heart attack in a suburban home. A man lay dead in the bathtub while his wife, pale-faced, but resolutely composed, answered questions put to her by the police in the entrance hall. Regulations determine that all instances of people dying of what appear to be unnatural causes be investigated by the police. Thus, it happened that another detective and I dutifully examined what appeared to be an innocent incident; yet something was amiss.

"Do you notice the color of his skin?" I asked my partner, as we stood back, assessing the situation. He looked at the fellow, sprawled out in the bathtub and then back at me before agreeing that something was definitely wrong. When someone dies, gravity takes over and the blood tends to collect under the skin at the lowest part of the body. This man, however, despite having supposedly died sitting upright in the tub, was covered in cherry-red blotches all over his body.

"Carbon monoxide poisoning?" my partner asked, the realization hitting us both at the same time. We were both familiar with the unique skin coloration indicating that someone had died from toxic exhaust fumes. "Then that would make this a set-up!"

The evidence from the post-mortem and investigation of the crime scene later indeed revealed that the man's wife had hit him on the head with a shovel and dragged him to the garage, where she gassed him in the family vehicle. She then lugged the body back to the bathroom, for what she imagined amounted to the perfect crime. This proved the saying often used in the cop shows: "People lie, but the evidence doesn't!" I loved this part of my job.

Those were turbulent times in South Africa. Apartheid, the political system of "separateness" that had been enforced by the government years earlier, was now an entrenched part of South African society. Where you were allowed to travel, what jobs you could do, where you could live and attend school and even whom you could marry were all enforced by law and determined by the color of your skin. In the decade of the 1980s in which I became a police officer, we increasingly saw violent clashes between those in power, represented by people like me, and those who had been oppressed for many years. There were weekly news reports of bombings, attacks and fiery conflicts in the townships and sometimes I would have to attend the scenes of vicious disputes in the course of duty.

There was no denying the horror of what I had become accustomed to seeing while on the job day after day. Betrayal, abuse, devastation and deceit confronted us regularly; but to me, the horror of some aspects of the job could not compare with the joy of piecing together the puzzle and trying to bring to light what was being hidden in darkness.

Not everyone, however, shared the same enthusiasm for my career of choice. "You smell like death," Petro, my wife, once muttered in disgust as she pulled back from embracing me on my return from work. She headed back to the kitchen, glancing over her shoulder with a scowl. "You smell like death, Martin – again."

It was probably true. I had investigated a dreadful case that day: a supposed suicide that had left a young, beautiful teenage girl dead on the living-room carpet with a bullet wound to the head, a handgun held limply in her hand and a mother, bewildered and screaming, in the dining-room. Yet, upon investigation, we had discovered gunpowder residue not on the girl's hands, but on her mother's.

My relationship with Petro was tumultuous, to say the least. She was my childhood sweetheart, the most gorgeous woman I had ever met, and as pragmatic as I might have thought I was, our love was of the "at first sight" variety.

She, with her long blonde hair and striking green eyes, was a member of the high school marching band and I played lead drum in the band. I doubt she would ever have noticed a guy like me – greasy and pimply in the unflattering drummer's uniform – but I guess my friends had seen me making eyes at her, because it wasn't long until, in true adolescent style, the dares began. I endured a few weeks of relentless teasing until I finally worked up the courage to follow her home from school one day.

That was about as far as I got for four days.

Eventually, having honed my stalking skills for close to a week, I managed to corner her on the way home from school one afternoon, introduced myself and asked her out to a movie. It was the craziest thing I had ever done, but sometimes, desperate times call for desperate measures.

I will never forget the way the surprised expression on her face faded, revealing a daring grin, before she accepted my brave proposal with a quick "Okay, as long as you ask my mother!" and flounced her way home. Her mother, although reluctant at first, gave her permission, and Petro and I made our first public appearance as a couple during the next weekend. We dated for several years before I again, with hands shaking and sweat beading on my brow, asked her another question, this time with a gold ring to seal the deal. Ever the suave gentleman, I rented not only a trendy white tuxedo, but also a stretch limousine, for a classy night out in town. Over dinner at the State Theatre in Pretoria I gently asked her to marry me and to my amazement she agreed, a bright smile lighting up her face.

However, as I now stood in the hallway of our Pretoria home, still hurting from her remarks about my police career, I realized that our relationship was no longer as harmonious as during those first few blissful years. Despite loving each other deeply, we struggled with conflicting flaws of character. I was stubborn at the best of times and this, together with low self-esteem, gave me the proverbial "chip on the shoulder". She was insecure and felt a pang of jealousy whenever I happened to glance at another woman. She would withdraw from me, absorbed in her own private hurt. For my part, I would sometimes explode in anger, once getting so infuriated that I managed to smash the windscreen of our car with my bare fist. Despite our problems, we took our vows – in which we committed ourselves to each other in marriage – seriously, especially in view of the fact that they were made before God.

Petro and I had both grown up in religious homes, with

church attendance and involvement in the local congregation a deeply ingrained part of our lives. For South Africans of my social background in that particular era, Christianity was almost more of a cultural exercise than a personal matter. Every Sunday, Mom would scrub the children's faces, smooth our hair and then, dressed in our finest threads and with cheeks still stinging red, we would be escorted down to the local church. My sister and I attended Sunday school with all the other children in our area and faithfully learnt our weekly Bible verses, but I don't remember the gospel ever meaning much more to me than simply obeying God's rules, turning up at church whenever possible, and keeping my face clean.

That all changed when I was about seventeen years old. Ironically, I was attending a course on evangelism when the Lord finally pointed out to me what salvation was all about. As the guest speaker explained in simple terms how we could communicate the good news to others, God broke through to my stubborn heart and it finally all made sense. I went home after class, got down onto my knees and made a commitment to the Lord Jesus to follow Him. Suddenly, God was no longer an abstract concept to me, but a very real and close friend, guiding me in my daily life. Petro, whom I had already been dating for some time, soon made the same commitment to Jesus. Completely transformed, we became sold-out "freaks" for Jesus. There was nothing we wished for more than to dedicate our lives to God in the same way that Jesus had done.

Somehow, though, despite having followed the Lord for so many years, things were not as clear-cut now, both spiritually and otherwise in my married and working life, as they had been in our youth. Sighing, I followed Petro into the kitchen, where she was unhappily rinsing lettuce under the tap in the sink. I leaned against the doorframe and watched her for a while, sensing the tension in the air, but not sure how to resolve it.

"What am I supposed to do, Penguin?" I pleaded, resorting to the endearing nickname I tended to use in tense moments like these.

She didn't reply, still concentrating on the lettuce, but responded to my remark with a slight shrug of the shoulders.

"I can't just quit my job. We need the money, and I would never be able to find something else that pays as well. Anyway, if I didn't have that work camera there is no way we could make all that extra cash on the side taking pictures at weddings…"

She glanced at me over her shoulder for a moment, a slight smile playing on her lips as she raised an eyebrow at me. "Those fancy brides wouldn't pay nearly so well if they knew that, only hours earlier, you'd been taking pictures of corpses with the same camera."

"I don't plan on telling them. Do you?" I quipped, wandering over and planting my hands on the kitchen counter next to her. I turned to her again and more seriously said, "I'm good at my job. And I'm pretty sure the Lord is happy with the influence I have on the other officers in the force."

It was true. I was upfront about my faith with my colleagues, and downright brash on occasions. I had even been known to corner a superior every so often and clearly explain to him the need for repentance and faith in Christ. God gave me great boldness in speaking out for Him to the people with whom I worked, as well as discipling a few new believers among them.

Petro nodded. "Just consider it, though. What if the Lord wants to do something new in your life? Let's just say I wouldn't be all that unhappy to have you home some evenings and to get rid of that awful stench which follows you everywhere."

"Fair enough, but He'd have to tell me pretty clearly if He wanted me to be convinced!"

Little did I know just how seriously God intended to take me at my word.

Chapter 2

I pace when I have my daily devotional time with Jesus. It is not an angry pacing, or the result of feeling constrained, like a lion trapped in too small a cage. Rather, I walk the room daily with the Lord from a determination to sort things out between us, trying to hear Him clearly and entreating His presence in my life.

It was early one morning during one of these intense times of deep reflection, while I was doing some kind of prayer walking around the coffee table, that the Lord gave me the clear confirmation I hadn't even meant to ask of Him.

Bible held open across my outstretched hands, I figured that the first chapter of Romans was as good a place to begin that morning as any other. Not for the first time, I began to read the opening salutation of the dispatch Paul had sent to the Christians in Rome: "Paul, a servant of Christ Jesus, called to be an apostle and set apart for the gospel of God."

While this was what was written clearly in bold typeface on the page in front of me, I read something completely different. "Martin," it proclaimed, "a servant of Christ Jesus, called and set apart."

I stopped, stunned, on the well-worn track in the carpet

between the couch and the bookcase. I read the verse again, trying to understand, again hearing the unmistakable voice of the Lord: "Martin, called to be an apostle." I was Jesus Christ's servant? Jesus Christ had called me?

His call was unmistakable. I knew with certainty at that moment that the Lord was calling me, like Paul, into full-time ministry. But, just as soon as I had heard His voice, I began to doubt. Who was I to be chosen for something like this? I was a police officer, not a pastor! What does someone in the ministry do, day after day, anyway? Thoroughly confused, I began pacing again, resolutely begging the Lord to give me clarity.

I guess the Lord can be just as stubborn as I am at times, because over the next few weeks, He spoke to me through a number of dreams, again confirming that He had chosen to call me for His own purposes. Strangers at church would approach me and ask me if I had ever considered quitting my job to work for God. Had I considered it? Nothing had ever weighed so heavily on me!

I tried to appease God by beginning a one-year correspondence course in theology. It was tough staying committed to my studies while still working full time in the police force. I learnt a great deal, and yet I sensed that this wasn't good enough. God wanted more, but I still wasn't sure if I was ready to take that step.

One afternoon, my father and I were spending some time together where we had both always felt most comfortable – in the garage, tinkering with the car. Things hadn't always been easy between Dad and me. He and Mom had quarreled bitterly when I was a child. I had resented his frequent absences, when he left us for days at a time to let the tensions in our home cool down before coming back again. However, since he had committed himself to the Lord some time previously, things between us had improved a great deal. As we chatted to each other, catching up on the latest news, Dad moved about the car, inspecting and fiddling, before finally settling onto his back under the chassis of our old Opel Rekord. Every so often, he would grunt from under the car, either in response to one of my stories, or in disgust at the state of the brake pads.

I cleared my throat, wondering how he would react when I broke the news. "Uhm, Dad? Petro and I have been kind of thinking of quitting our jobs…"

I saw him pause under the car, and then slowly slide his way out to look me in the eye. "Oh?"

"Yes. We've been praying about it for a while now, and we've decided… well, we think the Lord might want me to go into full-time ministry as a pastor."

My dad didn't say anything for a moment; he just lay there quietly on his back, looking at me with this strange expression on his face. He took a deep breath, and then replied, "I know."

"You know?"

Then he was crying on the garage floor, tears coursing down his face. For a few moments, he lay there, trying to compose himself. I could do nothing but, like an idiot, stare at him in silence, trying to figure out just what had brought on this unusual display of emotion. He sat up and came to sit next to me against the wall. Mystified as I was, I couldn't help but enjoy the closeness I felt with him at that moment, as he began to explain himself.

"The night you were born, I called your grandparents to give them the good news. They were so excited – you were the first grandson, you know – and they jumped straight into the car and drove six hours through the night to come and see you at the hospital in Pietermaritzburg.

"I couldn't figure what all the fuss was about. You were

quite an ugly baby." He looked me straight in the face, his eyes twinkling mischievously through the tears. "Born backside first into the world, causing your mother terrible pain, like you were just trying your best to cause a scene."

I grinned at him and he continued.

"And then your grandparents came bustling into the ward, while your mother was still trying to recover. They were godly people, but they could be really blunt at times…"

"Runs in the family," I joked.

Dad chuckled and then continued. "Your grandpa took you into his arms, and cradled you there so gently, looking intently into that wrinkled little face of yours. Then he said the most incredible thing: 'The Lord has told me to anoint this boy for full-time ministry.' Right there in the ward, he poured oil onto your forehead, prayed for you and told me to wait and see that the Lord would do what He had promised. So I guess you could say I'm not all that surprised by what you're telling me today."

"Wow," was about all I could mutter.

"I'm proud of you, son. And you may know you have your mother's and my full blessing as you take this next big step."

In a way more perfect than I could have asked for, God gave me the confirmation that I was on the right track. My choice would demand a great deal of sacrifice and faith, and yet I had real certainty that the Lord was guiding my path. A few weeks later, I handed in my resignation from the police force, much to the amazement of my friends there, and Petro quit her job, trusting that God would provide for us and allow her to be a full-time homemaker. I enrolled at the South African theological college of the AFM (Apostolic Faith Mission), and worked at odd jobs to support Petro and myself. We had faith that the Lord would provide the rest.

I was the first person in my family to study at tertiary level and I was determined both to please them and, in obedience to God, to complete my studies with as much gusto as I could muster. In class, I steadfastly sat through all of the regular theological school subjects – Hebrew and Greek, Old and New Testament surveys, counseling and children's ministry. I grew quickly in my understanding of theology and the skills required for ministry and got along well with the many other equally ambitious students. Outside of the lecture halls, however, the Lord was putting Petro and me through another set of lessons – those offered by the school of faith.

I don't think I had quite anticipated just how costly it would be to study. Books and other study materials were exorbitantly expensive and other living expenses, which just could not be covered in full by my meager part-time incomes, began to pile up. Over the first few months at Bible College, our small savings nest-egg, which we had so carefully accumulated, began to dwindle quickly.

These were difficult times for Petro and me. I would be at school from early in the morning until mid-afternoon and in the evenings went out packing shelves in warehouses and loading trucks until the very early hours of the morning, after which I would catch a few hours of much-needed sleep before beginning the whole cycle over again. Just getting out of bed in the mornings was a battle, but I was motivated to get to work again by the equally large piles of bills and homework stacked by my bed. I even stooped so low as to take on a job delivering summonses when things got really tough. This, of course, was a particularly unpleasant form of employment. We never seemed to get ahead financially and sometimes even came close to being completely penniless. Yet, time and again, the Lord provided. I remember reading Psalm 62:8: "Trust in him at all times, O people; pour out your hearts to him, for God is our refuge." The Holy Spirit spoke to me and encouraged me to trust in nobody else but God for providing our needs.

I remember realizing on several occasions at the end of the month that there was not enough money in our bank account to pay the rent of our tiny inner-city apartment. Petro and I would pray together, but keep our needs a secret from other people. That evening, stuck under our door, we would find an envelope with the word "Rent" scrawled on it, containing just enough cash to cover our costs. This happened several times. On other, similar occasions, we would discover a basket full of groceries in front of our door, just when our fridge was particularly empty. We never discovered who it was that had helped us out at just the right time, especially since we had never even made our needs public. This, of course, just made it easier to see that it was the Lord, and nobody else, who was taking care of us.

God looked out for us in other interesting ways as well. One of the part-time jobs I worked at to supplement my income was helping a friend who owned a butcher's shop. He paid me not in money, but in meat! Even though we were craving fresh vegetables at times, we at least had enough steak, chops, chicken fillets and *boerewors* (a very popular South African farm-style sausage) to satisfy our appetites. Sometimes our fridge would be so full of meat that we would trade it for other groceries and fresh food from friends!

Then the Lord taught me more about Himself through a new and interesting period of my life: fatherhood. Martin Junior was born in January 1992, my last year at Bible College. Now we were no longer only Martin and Petro, but a family! I was elated by the arrival of my new son and was a very proud dad, but suddenly I was faced with the pressures of being the only bread-winner, on a very limited income, for a family of three. The temptation to look first of all to myself to care for and protect this little one was very strong, but the Lord helped me learn a valuable lesson through that as well.

One evening, I was woken up by Martin's crying and as I needed to go to the bathroom, I told Petro that I would get up and see to him. Stumbling along the dark passage, I made my way to his room to comfort him – and found myself face to face with a burglar trying to break in through the window! I'm not sure which of the two of us was more startled, but the hapless robber took off quickly back through the window. I was reminded that God intended to care for and protect my little family, even when I felt completely incapable of carrying out that gigantic task.

As we grew in our trust of the Lord, I began to sense that He was busy revealing a plan for our lives that was very different from the one I had expected. At the time I had started at Bible College, I understood "full-time ministry" to mean becoming a pastor. I therefore oriented my life and goals in that direction. Among my friends at the college, the overriding ideal was to get a calling to a large, suburban church and then pastor the congregation there. However, as I came close to completing my studies, I began to hear stories of work in the mission fields and the need for the gospel in remote parts of the world. I became aware of other fields just as ripe for the harvest as those in my native South Africa.

I had never been very interested in missionary activity, until I had a very vivid dream one night. In the dream, Petro and I were saying goodbye to Africa, boarding a plane and flying to some far-off country to preach the gospel. I woke up in a sweat, and fell to my knees beside the bed, crying out to the Lord, "Please, Jesus! Don't send me away from South Africa. This is my home! I love my country. I am willing to go to the remotest part of this nation to work for You, only please don't send me away from here."

Again, I was confronted with an experience through which I could sense that God wanted to speak into our lives and guide us, just as we had always asked Him to do – yet here I was, refusing to listen to Him. God had brought global missions to the forefront of my mind in an instant, yet initially I did not want to have anything to do with an idea which might drag me away from the only country I had ever known.

As I studied the word of God, I discovered a very different attitude in Abraham. Here was a man who was also asked to leave his homeland and embark on a "mission" to an unknown part of the world for the glory of God. Here was a man worshiping foreign idols, living his own life and doing his own thing; but, when the God who made heaven and earth spoke to him, he got up, left everything behind and set off on an incredible journey of obedience to God. Who was I, a supposedly faithful servant of God, to refuse to consider following the Lord where He wanted to lead me?

About this time, I was sitting in a lecture at Bible College, when our professor began to describe to us the life of Jonah, the "reluctant missionary", who tried to escape the will of God, but kept being drawn back to the divine task God had appointed him to do. It had taken a torrential storm, near mutiny on the high seas and an excursion in the belly of a big fish to get through to him. In the end, Jonah realized that there was no possibility of hiding from the omniscient God. What a Jonah I was! There in the lecture hall, I submitted myself in prayer to the Lord and told Him that I was at least willing to consider the new direction into which He was leading me.

Much to the amusement of my friends at college, I began to talk seriously about heading for the mission fields rather than taking up a secure pastorate in a South African church. Even more intriguing to them was my sudden interest in the Muslim people living and working in the neighborhood around our Bible College. I don't know why I hadn't noticed them earlier, but suddenly I was aware of this whole other community living, working, going to school, sitting in the coffee shops and frequenting the mosque close to us, all without the knowledge of a Savior who loved them and had died for them.

Intrigued, I one day decided to head to the mosque down the street and see for myself what Islam was all about. Probably committing every cultural *faux pas* possible, I wandered through the huge carpeted hall with the local Imam (a Muslim spiritual leader) and discussed with him my own views about spirituality, salvation and faith. As usual, I expressed my arguments assertively, trying to convert this old man in his long, flowing white cloak and interesting hat. With an equal lack of tact, the Imam countered my arguments, just as unsuccessfully trying to convince me of his point of view. I remember quizzing him in frustration in my efforts to find out just what Islam was about.

Fingers stroking his beard lightly, the Imam's eyes suddenly lit up as he said, "I think I have just the thing to help you!" Hurrying to his bookshelf, he pulled out an enormous Quran, its cover decorated with beautiful swirled patterns and flowing Arabic script. Eagerly, the Imam showed me how this copy of the Quran contained both the original Arabic text and an English translation. Wishing me well, the old man suggested I read the ancient words in the book and learn from them.

I indeed learnt much from that Quran, but perhaps not the lessons that the Imam had intended for me. As I compared the Muslim holy book to my own inspired and living word of God, the Bible, I couldn't help but develop a deep compassion for the many millions of people around the world who are deceived by the teachings of Islam. Rather than drawing me closer to the Muslim faith, reading the Quran opened my eyes to the deceptive heart of Islam and helped me to better understand the beliefs of the Muslims around me.

With slightly more sensitivity than I had at first, I actively began evangelizing the Muslim people on the streets of Johannesburg. I drew those that I encountered into conversation, explaining to them the hope that Christ offers us through His work on the cross. Measured against worldly standards, I didn't have a great deal of success. There was no long line of well-discipled converts whom I could proudly show off at church on Sunday, but I went out boldly each week, knowing my job was simply to walk in obedience to God and trust Him with the fruit of my labors.

In the frenzy of final year exams and assessments, this burden of missionary work and reaching out to Muslims was growing in me daily. I also experienced a great deal of uncertainty about my family's future. Then I attended a talk given by a faculty member who had just returned from an exposure trip to the Middle East.

"Turkey!" the lecturer exclaimed, loading the first slide into the projector and pointing at the picture of a vast city-scape filled with the unmistakable domes of mosques. "A country with a population of 62 million, but with only 500 Christians among a majority of Muslims."

My heart began to race, and I leaned forward in my seat to listen more closely to the captivating speaker.

"One of the least reached nations on earth, my friends, and with only a few hundred missionaries to reach the masses. It used to be a region well saturated by the gospel, but now many there have never before even heard the name of Jesus."

This was it! My calling, lit up in a few blurry holiday

pictures by a slide-projector against the wall of the lecture theater. The deepest stirrings of my heart were finally exposed and expressed by this energetic man telling stories of a nation where just speaking the name of Jesus was enough to get you killed. Ecstatically, I ran up to the lecturer after class and shared my feelings with him. He, just as enthusiastically, thumped me on the back and promised to help me find my way.

In a cloud of dreams, I made my way home to Petro that evening, alternately grinning and then managing to compose myself enough to drive a little bit less like a maniac through the crazy Johannesburg traffic. Sweeping through the front door to meet my wife, I caught her up in my arms and, without a moment's hesitation, informed her that the Lord was calling us to Turkey.

I'm not sure if it was the way Petro tensed up in my arms, or the shocked expression on her face, which reminded me that sometimes occasions such as these required a little bit more sensitivity and less candor than I sometimes adopted.

"Where did this come from?" she asked, amazed, pulling back from my embrace and looking me in the face. "Turkey? I don't even know where that is!"

"Don't worry about that for now," I soothed, a little bit more calmly now. "But just think! A whole country full of Muslims for us to share the gospel with and only…"

Petro held up her hand to silence me and then very deliberately made her point: "I'm sorry, Martin, but you can forget it. I'm not leaving South Africa. I'm not going to some far-away place without my family and friends."

Crestfallen, it was all I could do to keep standing upright. I was stunned by the realization that my wife was not supporting me in what had – in the space of one afternoon – become the passion of my life.

"I'm sorry, Martin. I can't," she repeated slowly, carefully.

Disappointment was replaced by the all-familiar anger with which I had struggled since childhood, swelling in my heart. My hands instinctively clenched, and I fought the desire to lash out and force compliance from my wife. How could she deny me this opportunity to follow God's call, especially since it had taken me so long to become willing to obey?

Suddenly, though, my anger was drowned out by a flood of God's peace. With the wisdom only the Holy Spirit can provide, I realized that dragging my wife kicking and screaming to Turkey was just as wrong as being disobedient to His call in the first place. If this was truly from God, it was a calling not only on my life, but my whole family's lives. I would just have to trust the Lord to bring Petro around and convince her of this in His own time.

"Okay," I managed to reply, pulling Petro back into an embrace. "If you're not ready, then I'm not going anywhere."

Over the next few months, I wrestled with God in prayer, alternating between resting calmly in His peace that surpasses all understanding and anxiously begging God to hurry up with what I thought He needed to do. Daily I brought our situation before the Lord and pleaded that He would change Petro's heart so that we could move forward in unity. It was incredibly frustrating. In my head I trusted that if the Lord really wanted us in Turkey, He would help Petro to see it too; but some days it was difficult to make my heart feel the same way.

I'm not sure how much longer the carpet around our coffee table would have held up had it not been for a miraculous answer to prayer. One evening during our dinner of the usual bountiful fare of meat, Petro suddenly informed me that she was not only willing to follow me to Turkey, but in fact even wanted to go! Sensing that this was God's call on both of our lives, she was perhaps – almost – as eager as I was to leave our home turf and head out to the mission field.

Immediately, we gathered as much information as we could about different missionary guilds and sending organizations which might help us find our way to Turkey. Soon after we had begun our research, we stumbled upon information about OM, or Operation Mobilisation. We learnt that OM started out as a missionary movement in the 1950s when a group of college students from the United States tried to reach people in Mexico with Christian literature. What had begun as an enthusiastic – albeit slightly haphazard – movement to Latin America initiated by young people soon evolved into a worldwide, well-recognized mission organization. It became an institution which was better organized, but was still characterized by the youthful fervor which had set it apart in the early days. OM served in more than 100 countries in the world and had two ocean vessels, the *Logos* and the *Doulos*. We were most excited to learn that they also had a thriving church planting ministry in Turkey. It seemed like a perfect fit, but we were soon to be confronted by some slightly disconcerting information regarding OM.

"I'm sure your family would fit in well with the team in Turkey," the eager recruiting coordinator at the OM head offices in Pretoria informed us with a grin. "There are many other young families serving there and even though the ministry can be demanding, I'm sure someone with your qualifications would find it quite exciting."

"How soon can we go there?" I joked, rewarded with a swift kick under the table from Petro.

Our OM friend nodded, seemingly unfazed by my unbridled eagerness. "Oh, very soon. You'll have to complete six months of training first, but then, provided you have enough money to buy a plane ticket for the three of you, you can go there immediately after that."

"You mean OM won't provide the plane ticket?" I asked, a little perturbed.

"Generally, no," he answered. "Actually, you do realize that OM doesn't provide any finances for their missionaries, don't you?"

"Your missionaries aren't paid?" After years of trusting God to feed us from month to month, Petro and I had been looking forward somewhat to the idea of a stable income. "Does that mean we will need to work at part-time jobs to support ourselves living in Turkey?"

"Perhaps," he assented, "although you will be extremely busy just with the responsibilities of the ministry. You may need to have some kind of employment in Turkey in order to be granted a visa, but you will, of course, mainly focus on church planting. Which means the finances will have to come from somewhere else…"

He let that statement hang while Petro and I waited on the other side of the table in the pregnant silence. Conspiratorially, he leaned across the table towards us, his fingers intertwined in a steeple under his chin.

"The finances will have to come from God," he said triumphantly.

Having trusted the Lord to supplement our income through college, this was perhaps not as frightening a thought as it could have been. Still, did we have the faith to believe that the Lord would provide an amount as large as our complete income, every month, every year, for however long He called us to live in Turkey?

"If you can't trust God for a small amount of money, how will you be able to trust Him for the souls of lost people?" our advisor continued. "Share with your friends and family, and with your church, what God has called you to. Pray – a lot! Then, every month, you'll just have to have faith that God will work in the right hearts to send you the resources you need to do His work in Turkey, a country across a continent from South Africa."

On receiving this incredible information, all Petro and I could do was to nod and smile politely. This would indeed be one of the biggest leaps of faith we had ever taken. We realized, however, that if we truly wanted to be obedient to God's calling on our lives, it was a step of faith we needed to take. Just as we had seen God provide for us in the past, we would need to trust that He would not choose to abandon us now.

Sure enough, as we told our story to people we knew, we generally received their total support. Some promised to pray for us; others encouraged us and spoke words of inspiration and challenge, while some promised to support us financially. By God's grace, our mission to Turkey became a team effort encompassing the assistance of many people in different ways. We received invitations from churches in cities across South Africa to come and share our passion with the people in their congregations. In return, they shared their resources with us. In a very short time, God had provided enough donations and promises of help in the future to set us off on our journey to Turkey. It was still going to be difficult, knowing that we would be many thousands of kilometers away from the people who had pledged in various ways to stand alongside us. Yet we had confidence that this was no challenge to the Lord who ultimately holds all the finances and resources on earth in His very capable hands.

There was, however, a slightly more pressing challenge to be faced before the financial situation became much of an issue: missionary training.

I'm not sure what we expected to find at a missionary training center when we drove down the dirt road leading to the OM base outside Pretoria that first evening. Certainly, the small thatched cabins with peeling paint and dusty windows in which we would be living for the next six months looked like something at which Livingstone himself might have turned up his nose. Ablution facilities were simple, at best, and it was better not to attempt washing in the below-zero temperatures of winter-time if the warm-water system wasn't working. This unfortunately occurred regularly, often resulting in some rather unsavory odors in the classroom. In the mid-year dry season, we were threatened by grass fires, which hungrily consumed the parched grasslands surrounding the property. When the rains came, we would sometimes find ourselves ankle deep in red mud, and a water feature, which developed spontaneously, would gush through the ceiling of the dining-hall. We washed our laundry by hand, and never drank the last mouthful of a cup of tea in order to avoid the crunchy calcium deposits that flowed from our water tap and tended to settle at the bottom of whatever we wanted to drink.

Yet we made a home for ourselves in this very uncomfortable place. We were so encouraged to be among people who shared our passion for the lost people throughout the world, and traded stories of the humorous reactions we had experienced when we shared our goals in life with people.

While what I had learnt at Bible College had been valuable, here the teachings challenged my heart and not merely my mind. We were all encouraged to walk in daily communion with the Lord and to ask Him to bring to light any unresolved issues in our lives which might hinder our work in the mission field.

On the home front, Petro masterfully turned our small,

two-roomed cottage into a cozy haven for the three of us with colorful curtains and pictures on the walls. Our rooms were sparsely furnished, but this was probably a good thing, considering we really only had enough space for a bed and a few other small articles, including Martin Junior's crib.

Even though we shared communal dining facilities, sometimes Petro and I would withdraw from the crowd to cook for our little family. One rainy Saturday morning, Petro offered to make pancakes for little Martin and me. Happily, I helped with the preparations, only to discover we didn't have cinnamon to go with the sugar we liked to sprinkle over our warm pancakes. Still absorbed in the complicated process of flipping and frying, Petro shooed me off to go and beg some from one of our neighbors.

I was halfway to the little caravan that they called home when I realized I wasn't sure of the English word for cinnamon. There were people from all different languages and cultures at the OM training facilities and it was generally required of us to communicate only in our team language – English. Petro and I had studied English briefly at school, but we were only barely proficient in speaking the language. In the staunchly Afrikaans-speaking community of Pretoria at that time, this had not been such an issue. Now we were quickly beginning to realize that life on the mission field might require a slightly higher level of competency in this complicated language. Screwing up my courage, I decided to give it my best shot anyway and, knocking on our neighbors' door, repeated quietly to myself the polite request I intended to make.

I will never forget the look of horror on my kind friend's face when I courteously requested to borrow her bottle of semen! That particular morning, as Petro and I laughed over our cinnamon pancakes, we resolved to work very hard at becoming fluent in English!

We had some amazing experiences while in training and were often reminded of God's faithfulness and His commitment to us as a family. Within the first few weeks, we were to be sent on an outreach to a very rural area of South Africa. There we would participate in ministering to refugees from Mozambique, who had escaped the civil war by fleeing through the Kruger National Park. Martin Junior was joining us on the outreach and Petro was feeling unsure of how she would manage the thankless task of washing diapers while living in a tent, with no electricity and very limited access to water. Like the rest of the women in the village, she would have to stand in a queue for up to an hour every day to collect a large bucket of water, and then lug it back up the hill to our campsite. We would have loved to be able to purchase disposable diapers, but our limited income made the cost of this prohibitive. We decided to commit this need to the Lord in prayer.

The night before we left on the outreach, I noticed in amazement as a pair of car headlights made its way along the main road outside the training base, before turning into our driveway and bouncing across the bumpy track to where I was busily trying to pack our baggage into the car. Thinking that whoever was driving had to be lost, I wandered over to the driver's window, preparing to give directions. Instead, as the window rolled down, a woman hesitantly leaned out and enquired if people named Martin and Petro lived there.

Intrigued, I confirmed that I was the person she was looking for. Relieved, the woman jumped out of the car and began taking box after box of disposable diapers out of the trunk. Not quite believing my eyes, I just watched as she unloaded several weeks' supply of this precious commodity, wished me well and got back into her car to drive away into the evening. To this day, I have no idea who the woman was, or even how she knew we needed diapers when we had not told a single person about it; yet we left for our outreach the next day praising God's goodness and with our small Volkswagen Golf loaded up to the ceiling with disposable diapers.

Our time in what was then the Gazankulu area of South Africa was life changing. We worked alongside the resident OM team in that area, doing evangelism and helping the local community in whichever practical ways we could. Perhaps even more memorable were the evenings, when our team would worship the Lord in song around the campfire, which was not merely there for ambience but was also used for cooking all our food.

One morning, after a particularly large fire had been made the previous evening, I sleepily emerged from our tent to see some of the coals still smoldering inside the circle of stones which marked out our hearth. Groggily rubbing my face, I thought that I should extinguish the remaining coals before Martin Junior woke up. I wandered away for a brief moment before a startled cry woke me from my morning haziness. There was Martin, just as I had anticipated, his little feet in the burning hot coals. Snatching him up, I threw him, feet first, into a bucket of water which, thankfully, was standing nearby, angrily cursing my stupidity and trying to soothe a screaming Martin at the same time. As others were woken up by the startling noise, they joined us at the bucket. I held my son and prayed that God would heal whatever damage had been done to his feet. When I pulled him from the water some minutes later, we were amazed to see that there was not a single mark on his delicate little soles. Previously, on the same day as we had received the "miracle diapers", Martin had reached out and touched the iron while Petro was busy ironing. His index finger had blistered immediately. Now, when the damage could potentially have been much worse, only a few stray tears and sniffles bore evidence of the incident a few minutes before. Once again, the Lord showed us that He cared for us and His hand was over us as a family.

Of all the lessons we learnt during our six months of training with OM, this was perhaps one of the most valuable. It was a truth we would need to cling to as we headed into the unknown and began a new life among the Muslim people in Turkey.

Chapter 3

I've learnt, the hard way, that it is best not to take travel advice from people who have never ventured farther than a few hundred kilometers from their home.

Back then, in 1993, as we prepared to uproot our little family and leave for Turkey, I was not nearly so wise. "Take as much baggage on the plane with you as you can," my mother had strongly suggested, with a knowing look in her eyes that only parents can muster. Just as naïve about international travel as she was, I had dutifully packed all our worldly possessions into the duffle bags that were now hanging precariously from our bodies as we stumbled through the international terminal building in Johannesburg. Exactly why we considered sleeping bags, picnic baskets and a vanity case filled with cosmetics to be helpful on our trip is still a mystery to me. With tearful goodbyes said, and the necessary paperwork collected, we shuffled towards our departure gate, my arms loaded with baggage, and Petro struggling to steer an overloaded baby stroller containing, somewhere beneath piles of various items, a slightly overwhelmed toddler.

I made it only as far as the doorway to the plane before realizing that there was no way I would be able to carry my whole load down the narrow aisle in one trip. Appealing to the better nature of one of the patient stewards at the entrance, I left half my load there and then hurriedly ushered Petro, Martin Junior and a couple of sleeping bags to our assigned seats. I bundled our luggage into the overhead compartments, and in great frustration urged Petro to take her seat. Little Martin, overwrought from the goodbyes and strange new environment, lifted his voice in a pitiful wail. People glared in my direction, annoyed that the crying should begin even before take-off, but I expertly stared them down, pushing my way back against the flow of traffic, muttering mumbled apologies when necessary and regretting my over-zealousness in packing. Determinedly lunging against the crush of passengers, I eventually emerged again at the doorway, and with a relieved sigh slung the remaining bags across my shoulders and tucked the folded stroller into the crook of my elbow. Somewhere in the rear of the plane, I could still hear Martin Junior alternately sobbing and hiccupping.

I was on the home stretch down the aisle, when the unthinkable happened. The thin, white strap attached to Petro's vanity case caught onto the shoulder of seat 26C. The metal clip opened. I was jerked backwards and, as if in a perfectly choreographed stunt, the case opened and flung its contents in a wide spray across the travelers in the surrounding rows of seats. As though in slow motion, I watched delicate little bottles of lotion and several pairs of Petro's favorite ear-rings roll teasingly under the seats. There was nothing to do but fall to my knees and fumble around to gather up our scattered belongings. The passengers held up behind me let out a collective, impatient groan and I felt my face reddening, my hands full of women's perfume. Tripping only once over the stroller, I managed to scrape everything back into the case and stumbled to our seats, where a harried and embarrassed Petro was trying to soothe our son while sinking down as low as possible into her place.

When faced with such situations, there's not really much of a choice; you have to either laugh or cry. Wiping a handkerchief across my sweating brow, I reached out to squeeze Petro's hand, met her eyes and let out a quiet chuckle. "Please, Lord – let it get easier from here on…"

Thankfully, that was the most upsetting aspect of our journey to Turkey. The farewells with family and friends had been difficult, but now that we were on our way, there was suddenly a real sense of relief and anticipation about what our future would hold in this unknown land.

Even if we did not know what to expect in Turkey, it was comforting, on our arrival, to discover that Turkey was expecting us. A tall, wiry missionary met us at the arrival gate in Ankara, his face stretched in a wide grin.

"Welcome!" he boomed, shaking my hand vigorously in both of his large ones and then enveloping Petro in a suffocating hug. Ian, from Canada, was to be our team leader in this new field, but it seemed there was to be no time for introductions there at the airport. Pinching Martin Junior affectionately on the cheek and then taking hold of our bags, our energetic host took off, leading us with long strides to the old brown station-wagon he had left parked outside.

During our car trip from the airport, I peered inquisitively at the unfamiliar landscape while Ian animatedly described life in the bustling Turkish capital city. Set in a rocky crater amidst the dry steppe of central Turkey, Ankara features prominently throughout the pages of history. The ancient Hittite civilization was based in this region and even today its history impacts on Ankara society. What was most interesting for me was that this city was once the capital of the Roman province of Galatia, where Paul traveled to preach the gospel. The early church here had been strong, spurred on by the challenging letter that Paul had written to them. Now, however, Islam had taken root and again Christian missionaries were traveling to the region to proclaim Christ.

Through the naked, undulating hills we drove, our very lives endangered every moment by the many other boxy, Italian-designed cars careering erratically along the highway. I soon learnt that the Turks, being an emotional people, drove as emotionally and out of control as they dealt with other matters in life.

Even compared to the less-than-tropical environment I was used to back home on the Highveld of South Africa, the landscape surrounding Ankara looked alien and barren, with nothing more than rough, brown grass to be seen for endless kilometers.

Before entering the main center of town, we drove through a *Gece Kondu*, the Turkish equivalent of a squatter camp, with hundreds of tiny, one- and two-roomed mud-brick houses clinging to the hillsides. The residents of the homes are given legal ownership privileges, provided the whole building is erected in less than twenty-four hours.

The sun had set and Petro and Martin Junior were dozing fitfully in the back of the car, before we finally arrived at the small apartment in the suburbs we were to call home during our orientation time in Turkey. We unfolded ourselves from the cramped little car and began unloading our baggage from the trunk. Ian continued to chatter away happily, but I couldn't help noticing the way he kept peering cautiously over his shoulder as though expecting someone to attack him at any moment.

"Expecting trouble?" I tried to sound confident, despite feeling nervous.

"Maybe," he commented, peering at me from under bushy eyebrows. "I've been arrested a few times recently, but tonight I'd really like to be home in time for bed."

While Petro slept next to me that night, I lay awake wondering just what kind of trouble I had signed us up for.

I must have dozed off eventually, because the next thing I remember was being awakened with a start by the mournful cry of a muezzin, wailing the morning call to prayer. One of the five pillars of Islam, prayer is considered an essential part of the Muslim lifestyle and is practiced with great dedication five times each day. In each mosque, a muezzin will shout (often, nowadays, with electronic amplification) from the minaret to notify the public of the approaching, carefully calculated, prayer time. Long considered by many to be almost an art form, the call of the muezzin would at times degenerate from its intended religious function into a competition of volume between neighboring mosques.

It was still dark, but I imagined the many millions of Muslims in homes around me who were now kneeling on prayer mats, offering up prayers to a God who could not see, hear or help them. Spurred on by that thought, I stood up and spent some time talking to my heavenly Father, thanking Him for our journey and then asking His help as we set out to become familiar with this city to which He had brought us.

Spiritually strengthened for the day, I set out in search of sustenance of a more physical kind. Outside our front door, a completely new world was bathed in early morning light. Multi-storied tenements rose above the main thoroughfare along which yellow taxis and overcrowded buses raced, horns blaring. Along the sidewalks, shop owners sat in the doorways of their dank establishments, smoking pipes, while men and women scurried about, obviously on their way somewhere important. Some women wore headscarves, but these were in strange contrast to the very fashionable, modern, Western clothes they were wearing. Men in thick jackets and dull-grey trousers spat onto the footpath as I wandered along. I noticed that nobody looked up to greet me or meet my eyes. Everyone seemed absorbed in his own world and wasn't particularly interested in this stranger wandering about, no matter how out of place he might have felt.

I managed to locate a small sidewalk kiosk, with breads and pastries of all shapes and sizes stacked haphazardly in baskets behind the counter. A ring-shaped pastry caught my fancy, and I would have politely enquired about the price had I been in command of enough of the Turkish language to express myself. English was not going to serve me very well in this particular establishment, let alone my home language, Afrikaans. I think it was only then that I truly realized just how necessary it would be to acquire the language in order to conduct my daily life in Turkey.

Using a combination of gestures and emphatic grunts, I managed to communicate my intentions to the shopkeeper, who unenthusiastically wrapped my breakfast in paper, and took the correct change from my outstretched hand. Triumphantly, I made my way home to my little family, resolving to celebrate this small success, even if it was as simple as purchasing our daily bread.

Over the next few days, I slowly became better acquainted with the narrow streets and alleys surrounding our new home. I enjoyed exploring the new terrain, and tried hard to pick up words and phrases in Turkish to make myself understood. Ian and a few other members of the Ankara team helped to introduce us to the way of life in Turkey, the strange new currency in which we had to bargain at the bazaars and some of the cultural nuances with which we would have to be acquainted if we were to avoid alienating ourselves from our neighbors. Three days a week, I attended language classes at the Ankara University, while Petro studied at home with a "language helper" from the community. Relying on English alone was simply not an option; if we wanted to connect with local people, we were going to need to be fluent in Turkish. Exposed to it daily, it did not take me long to begin picking up some of the basics of the language. We still made our fair share of mistakes, though. On one infamous occasion, on my daily visit to the bakery down the road, I stunned the shopkeeper, not with my new-found proficiency in Turkish, but with the bizarre request to purchase some fresh men! Petro too, on another occasion, amused waiters at a restaurant when she politely ordered a bowl of hot socks.

The small flat in which Petro and I were living was only a temporary solution to our accommodation needs and so most days on which I did not attend classes at the university, I would head out early with Chaneek, a Korean team-mate, to go house-hunting. I felt like a pioneer, taking the city buses to follow up on advertisements of available apartments in the paper, or walking along the road with face turned up looking for the *kiralik* signs posted high in the windows, indicating a home for rent. I would return home in the evenings to Petro, with a crick in my neck, but full of stories to tell about the amazing things I had experienced during the day. Somehow I failed to notice that Petro, after being cooped up with a small child at home all day, and afraid to venture outside into this new environment, was not nearly as enthusiastic about everything Turkey had to offer as I was.

The small, dank basement apartment in which we found ourselves living had become something of a prison to my normally outgoing wife. When she emerged at street level, on rare occasions, she only experienced muddy, melted snow (which would seep through her jeans and unsuitable trainers), unfriendly locals and grey buildings which blocked out the sunlight. Shopping for daily necessities was a traumatic, unpredictable business; making friends was nearly impossible. With just a TV, and the Turkish equivalent of *Sesame Street* to keep Martin Junior occupied during the day, she desperately begged me to find an alternative to our temporary, subterranean home and to do so quickly.

Eventually, I discovered the perfect place for us to live. It was a small apartment on the ground floor of a building, with a little garden at the back, just perfect for young Martin who, by now, always seemed to be wandering off somewhere. Set on a hill, we would there be able to escape from the smog and dust which menacingly hangs over the city in winter-time. Petro set to work expertly turning our apartment into a home, organizing everything according to our tastes.

Our landlords, an older couple called Kamil and Meryam, lived above us and seemed enchanted by Martin Junior. Our first conversation, with the aid of an English–Turkish dictionary, was exhausted within fifteen minutes; but, slowly, as we became more confident in the language, our discussions would last for much longer and we became very good friends.

It was Kamil and Meryam who introduced us to the delicate art of Turkish hospitality. Upon arriving at their home, we would be invited to remove our shoes and put on a pair of warm, comfortable house-slippers, which would be waiting for us inside the doorway. Then, after being politely ushered into the immaculately clean guest lounge, our hands would be shaken, cheeks kissed and we would be offered a few drops of lemon-scented cologne to rub onto our hands and cheeks.

As the fresh aroma of citrus pervaded the room, the

greetings would begin. Each guest would in turn be asked about the health of, not only our immediate family, but also our distant relatives. We, in turn, would make the same enquiries of our hosts. It tended to be quite a long process, especially when slowed down even further by the thoughtful chewing of the occasional handful of delicious nuts, served on small, silver trays. Nevertheless, it was an important part of the hospitality ritual and definitely not a waste of time, as it was during this conversation that the tea would be brewed.

Strong and flavorsome, Turkish tea is a drink to be savored and definitely not adulterated with milk, as it is in the West. Our hostess, who would watch over us like a hawk to ensure our cups were never empty, would serve it to us in small glasses. The minute the last drop would slide down our throats, she would immediately rise again, pouring another serving from her pot. Only when we took our teaspoons and balanced them across the rim of our glass would she relax, having made sure that our thirsts had been quenched.

Once this ritual had been completed, the important discussions would begin. Always loud, but never disrespectful, conversation would cover a wide range of topics. Sometime close to the end of our visit, we would be offered fresh fruit and strong coffee, before we were allowed to request permission from our hosts to leave. Out in the passage, we would find our shoes, arranged with toes facing the door. Our host would have slipped away sometime during the visit to do this. I loved the comfortable predictability of these little social customs, as well as the kind intent of the Turkish people to communicate their caring, even for foreigners like us.

Our home and social lives having been settled to my satisfaction, I now began itching to become involved in some kind of ministry. In most of Turkey it is *de facto* illegal to share the gospel. I could not just tell people that I was a missionary. Rather, I needed to have a cover, a legitimate reason, apart from evangelism, for being in the country. My official job title on documents for the Turkish embassy was that of liaison officer. I was the Turkish representative for a South African tour company investigating the possibilities of holidays to religious sites in the region. There was, of course, never any real intention for this tour company to send groups to my city. In fact, during my time in Turkey, the company back in South Africa went bankrupt – something I didn't feel obliged to tell the bureaucrats in Turkey. However, as long as my paperwork had been lodged with the authorities and the right forms had been rubber-stamped, my purposes for being in Turkey were accepted as valid.

However, now that I had set up this charade of being a liaison officer researching possibilities for religious tourism, I faced the dilemma of figuring out what it was, exactly, that a liaison officer did all day. My neighbors, in typical Turkish fashion, were very interested in my movements from day to day and intrigued as to why I, unlike all the Turkish men, did not leave for work early every morning and arrive home late in the evening. They weren't to know that my almost non-existent company couldn't afford to rent office space for me. So, to give the wagging tongues a rest, I began to rise early and, dressed neatly and with a briefcase in hand, leave home for work. I even grew a moustache.

What my neighbors didn't know was that my destination each day was a large park down the road, where, briefcase and all, I would sit and chat to people on the park benches. I developed the unique concept of a "losing" ministry, by which I would purposefully leave Bibles and tracts, wrapped in black plastic, on the benches and in buses for other people to pick up and read later. It only happened a few times that I was indiscreet enough to cause someone to come running up behind me to return my lost property. When I was particularly bored, I would feed the ducks. As long as I could maintain the semblance of being an important, busy businessman, I would be able to keep my neighbors happy. I chose not to see the forlorn expression on Petro's face each morning as she stood by the window and watched me walk through our front gate and up the street.

Even if not particularly effective business-wise, my daily outings were excellent opportunities for me to learn more about the culture and language of Turkey. Frequently, I would sit down to chat with some of the other people visiting the park during the day. We would progress through the usual pleasantries – "What is your name?", "Where are you from?" and "Why are you here?" – before I would be asked a question that really astounded me: "How much money do you earn and what rent do you pay?" At first, I felt very uncomfortable about this question and would mumble something incoherent before changing the subject. Soon, however, I learnt that the root of the inquiry lay deep within Turkish culture. Interactions between people in Turkey are governed by an unspoken but clearly recognized class system. Those who are your superiors and who earn more than you do deserve your respect. Those who are socially beneath you are ignored. In essence, my new acquaintances were trying to figure out how to relate to me. Over time, I discovered that, as often demonstrated by Jesus, it is sometimes best to answer a question with a question: "Why do you need to know my salary?" Otherwise, I would respond with the well-known Turkish proverb, "You don't ask a woman her age, and you don't ask a boss his salary…"

For months, my life continued in this pattern, with very little variation. Usually, I managed to maintain a level of enthusiasm for my routine, even if it was tedious. Every so often, however, I would allow the little doubts to surface. Shouldn't I have been engaged more in real missionary work by now? My language proficiency was increasing quite well and I had been able to share my testimony of salvation many times. Where was the fruit? Why had God brought me so far from home just to keep some ducks well fed?

My predictable schedule was interrupted every Tuesday when Ian, my indomitable team leader, and I would travel up to the forest outside the city to pray. He was a fierce intercessor, as resolute and passionate in his prayer life as he was in just about everything else he set out to do. I learnt a great deal about prayer from him. He spoke to the Lord as I did to my own father, with affection and joy, but sometimes with candor as he begged God to help him understand His will. He entreated the Lord for mercy on behalf of the many millions of people perishing in the city below us, without knowledge of His saving grace. Just as easily, though, he would laugh and share an amusing anecdote, or something special he appreciated that God had given him.

He was dedicated too. I remember praying knee-deep in snow on one occasion, my toes numbed and my clothes soaked through, wanting to head home and help myself to some hot Turkish coffee, but then catching a glimpse of the look of joy on Ian's face. He was no saint and made his fair share of mistakes, but here was a man after God's own heart, and one whom I could emulate.

One particular Tuesday, while I was walking and praying alone in the forest, something very unusual happened. Suddenly, a dragon, large and threatening, its eyes smoldering with hate and fixed on me, appeared in front of me. As though transfixed, I stood still, watching the fearsome creature moving towards me. I lifted up a plea to the Lord to save my life as the dragon lunged at me to swallow me whole, its mouth opened wide and its breath smelling of death. I cowered, but then looked up into the creature's jaws to see that it had no teeth at all.

Sweating and trembling, I awoke from what had been a vividly terrifying vision. I sat beneath a tree to rest my shaking limbs, and sensed God revealing the meaning of the vision to me: the evil one would attack me and he would attempt to harm me, but I would not be hurt. God's peace filled my heart as I rested against the rough bark of the towering pine and I thanked Him for speaking to me so clearly, although I didn't really understand what He was telling me.

When I had recovered sufficiently I raced back to Ian to tell him of the amazing experience I had had, as well as the warning I had received that a significant attack was going to be made on our lives and ministries. We prayed for a while longer and then, feeling satisfied that there was not much else we could do, we headed back for the city to begin our weekly Bible distribution exercise.

Handing out Bibles in Ankara is perhaps the closest I have ever felt to being a character in one of those old spy films we used to watch in the cinemas. With a Turkish New Testament or *Jesus* film hidden snugly in one of our coat pockets, we would discreetly make our way through the alleys and lanes of the inner city. There we would attempt to sell the literature to second-hand bookstores, or smuggle it to contacts who we knew were interested in the gospel. Then we would disappear into the crowded streets once again. Distributing evangelistic literature in Turkey was enough to get you locked up, or at least seriously roughed up and thrown out of the country, so it was important for us to be careful. On this particular Tuesday, we strolled cautiously to a rendezvous point where we had agreed to hand over some Christian resources to a new convert.

Suddenly, they were everywhere: police in dark-blue

uniforms as well as plain-clothes detectives milling in the road. Police cars were parked across the footpath, their blue lights rotating. Onlookers were leaning out of apartment windows, interested in all the fuss. Unwittingly, we had managed to wander right into the middle of a police blockade. A tough-looking officer accosted us and, yelling something in Turkish, grabbed me by the shoulder and dragged me to the side of the police car. Ian was also being dragged along next to me. Through the thick wool of the winter coat he was wearing I could feel the shape of the *Jesus* film video he had put into his pocket to give to our contact. This was enough to land us in serious trouble.

"Turn around and put your hands on the car!" one of the police officers ordered us. I knew what was coming; we were about to be searched and when they found the video tape we would be hauled off to jail. Yet, as I caught a glance of Ian's face, I remembered the vision that God had given me earlier that morning. "Remember the toothless dragon," I whispered.

He nodded slightly and quietly muttered under his breath, "Pray."

I saw the corner of the video sticking out of Ian's pocket, and groaned inwardly, but prayed anyway.

Suddenly, there was a shout. "Hey! What do you think you are doing?" A police officer, obviously of senior rank, hurried over to where we were just about to be searched. "Let these men go."

Our captors frowned and tried to explain themselves. "But sir! We suspect these men of smuggling Christian propaganda." There was the hint of a proud smirk on the face of one of them.

The official paused and responded coolly, "I said, let them go," before briskly turning and walking away, leaving some shocked colleagues and even more shocked law-breakers behind.

We were barely able to contain our relief and joy as we politely accepted the mumbled apologies of the police and continued on our way. Once we had safely turned the corner and had left the blockade behind, I let out a jubilant shout and exclaimed, "Can you believe it!"

Ian grinned, his huge white teeth gleaming. "Absolutely! That's my God!"

We rushed back to the team to share our amazing experience, praising God as we went. I was momentarily buoyed up from the feelings of doubt and uncertainty about our presence in Turkey that had been plaguing me for weeks.

Despite the spiritual high I experienced that day, I still struggled with a growing disappointment in God and tried to hide it from my colleagues. He had promised so much and we had given up so much for Him; yet I didn't see any visible return on the huge investment we had made. Still, I managed to maintain the usual confident façade that I had carried with me from childhood. Petro, on the other hand, while sharing in our joy upon hearing how the Lord had pulled us through, didn't hide her nagging doubts nearly as well as I did.

"Please don't go again," she asked me one day, as I was heading out of the door to go to "work". We had discovered that she was expecting our second child and, though we were very happy about it, she was struggling to keep up with a very active two-year-old while dealing with the pregnancy as well. "I feel so lonely during the day. Can't you stay just for a while to keep me company?"

"I've got things to do," I said confidently, though trying hard to remember anything that I was particularly busy with at that time. "Why don't you take Martin Junior to play with Kamil and Meryam?"

"I can't do that any more!" she cried. "Meryam won't speak

to me now that I won't let her play with Martin alone."

It was true. Little Martin had loved playing with his new Turkish grandmother during the day when Petro was busy around the house. What had been a welcome relief to Petro had become a real problem when we discovered Martin reciting Muslim prayers that Meryam had taught him.

"Well," I said, making my way to the door. I was running late for my appointment with nobody in particular. "Why don't you go out exploring, like I do? You might enjoy it."

"Martin! They think I am a Russian prostitute! They are the only other women in Turkey with blonde hair like mine. I can't stand the way the men in their shop-fronts look at me." Petro shuddered and I knew she was thinking about the many times that Turkish men had stared at her, lewd grins on their faces, or even worse, reached out to touch her in the bazaar.

"Please, Martin. Stay here with me. I don't know the language here. I don't know the people. I don't even like the people." She sighed. "I need your help, Martin. Can't you see how lonely I am?"

With the air of someone who knows he has the moral high ground, I smiled benevolently at Petro and reminded her that sometimes this loneliness was a price we had to be willing to pay as missionaries in Turkey.

She looked me in the face and said the unthinkable.

"Then I don't want to be a missionary any more. I want to go home."

I am still amazed at how puffed up with pride I had become. Without realizing it, I thought of myself as the great missionary and believed that God needed me alone to reach out to all of Turkey, even if it was at the expense of my wife and family. While I now know that my responsibilities as a missionary cannot outweigh my obligations as a husband and father, at the time I believed that the "call of God on my life" was a good excuse to neglect those closest to me.

That day, I managed to cajole my wife into believing that things would get better and decided to be of greater help to her on this journey. She was pregnant and hormonal, after all, and certainly deserving of a little more attention. For some time, my eyes having been opened, things improved and talk of going home was forgotten. I hope that from then on I indeed began to be more attentive to the needs of my family, realizing that things were perhaps tougher for them than I had liked to believe. However, even I seriously began to doubt whether God had really called us to this barren place.

The differences between our new home and the home in our hearts became more and more apparent as time went on. As difficult as life in South Africa could be at times, it was often far worse in Turkey. The fact that the people were spiritually lost really became too much for me to bear at times. I remember on one occasion sitting outside a McDonald's (Halaal, of course) outlet, waiting for a contact, watching the world go by. I saw thousands of feet hurriedly making their way somewhere. I was suddenly stunned by the thought that, in all likelihood, each of these pairs of feet was just as quickly stumbling towards hell. In a city of just over four and a half million people, only about a hundred knew Christ and the salvation He offered. The sheer size of the task, the enormity of the spiritual need, overwhelmed me. Here was a society offering financial security, with most people living in great material comfort, and yet, overall, it was spiritually bankrupt. Worse still, very often it felt as if there was little I could do about it.

There were other obstacles, too. Between my niggling qualms and Petro's huge belly, I wasn't getting much sleep at night and exhaustion was beginning to set in.

Having found a doctor who could speak some limited English, we were given the assurance that, in order to help with the translation both ways, I would be allowed to attend the birth, despite the fact that it was considered inappropriate in the Turkish culture. We therefore decided to stay and have the baby in Turkey. Our newest arrival, a boy, was to be a big baby and was in breach position just as his dad had been, so a C-section was scheduled.

With some nervousness, but even more excitement, we headed for the hospital on the day of the procedure in August 1994, ready to welcome our new family member into the world.

Petro, resolutely calm on the operating table, held my hand and chose not to be distracted by the bustling of medical staff and the unavoidable whispering we managed to elicit whenever we two foreigners were out in public. With a smile, we greeted our doctor and I helped to interpret the usual civilities before the big event got underway.

I'm still not exactly sure what went wrong. An anesthetist was there. I saw him administer the medication. However, as the surgeon reached for her scalpel, Petro gripped my hand and whispered frantically, "Martin! I'm not ready – I can still feel everything."

I felt a chill spread down my spine. I stared at her in mute terror for a moment, before pleading haltingly with the doctor, "Please, Doctor, stop! My wife – she is not ready. She can still feel everything!"

"She is nervous," she replied, slightly irritated, and then continued, "She will be fine," as she leaned down to begin her incision.

With the first cut, Petro cried out in pain. Though immobilized by the drugs, she could still feel every slice of the surgeon's knife. "Stop, please!" she begged, switching between English and Turkish and crying out in agony while I also pleaded with the doctor to stop. Had I not been afraid that a slip of her scalpel could cause more harm to my wife already lying in desperate pain on the table, I would have wrestled it from her hand. Instead, I yelled; but it seemed the louder I yelled, the more determined the doctor became to carry on.

Angered by my persistent yelling, she finally snapped, "Well, just tell her to hang on. I am nearly through," before Petro, overcome by the pain, finally fainted, still moaning softly.

Another wail broke through the heavy atmosphere in the operating theater. This time it was our son, Benjamin. He was put into my arms, serenely sucking a finger and observing the world with big eyes, seemingly unaware of the fuss his entrance into it had created. The doctor, a little less brusque now, ordered more pain medication and worked at stitching Petro up, while the nurses continued to regard us all in amazement, that a man was allowed to be privy to what was clearly meant only to be women's business.

When Petro eventually woke up and held her son for the first time, I had no doubt that, despite the trauma, she knew it had all been worth it. Our son, a big, happy, blond baby, was a blessing who softened some of the difficult memories we carried of that harrowing experience. The incident did little, though, to encourage us to persist in hanging on and sticking out the difficult times in Turkey. United by the ordeal, Petro and I seriously began to talk of leaving Turkey. I felt spiritually disappointed and let down by God, while a numbing depression overtook Petro and smothered her like a heavy blanket. Every time the planes flew over our little flat, I thought of how easy it would be to step aboard a jumbo and leave.

Our friends and colleagues encouraged us to persevere, and rightly so. They advised us to take a break, go on holiday. We felt so burnt out that even the idea of a holiday seemed exhausting to us.

Then suddenly, everything started happening so quickly. An Austrian family, who were joining the work in Ankara, offered to take over our lease, as well as to buy all our furniture. We took it as a sign. Tickets were purchased, loose ends tied and goodbyes hastily said. We were relieved to be leaving Turkey.

We felt like complete failures.

Chapter 4

There are definitely cleaner floors in the world, but it was with great excitement that I bent down and kissed the floor tiles in the Johannesburg airport terminal building, much to the delight of friends and family who had gathered to welcome us home. Petro grimaced and rolled her eyes at my antics before being engulfed in hugs, and family members separated her from our chubby new son who, with his protective older brother, quickly became the center of attention.

We were home, after two eventful years. Even as I struggled once again under the weight of all our worldly possessions in traveling bags, I couldn't help but realize that the emotional weight of caring for my family in another country was being lifted from my shoulders. Here, surrounded by the people we most loved in the world and in a familiar environment, I at last felt at peace. I looked across at Petro and saw the same relief on her face.

In tears, my mom fought her way through the crowd to wrap me in her arms. "I'm so glad you're home," she choked, her voice thick with emotion. "I thought we would never see you again!" This solicited chuckles from a few of the bystanders, except for my dad. Although he seemed pleased to see us, he had a grim expression on his face.

"Welcome back, son," he said gruffly, acknowledging my presence with a pat on my back. For a moment, it almost looked as though he wanted to say more, but instead he shrugged his shoulders and made way for the other, more cheerful, members of the welcoming party.

One of Petro's brothers wandered over to help pick up the bags. "Ah, well," he said, cheerfully enough. "The holiday's over, then. Time to get back to the real world."

Petro winced at his words, but didn't comment.

Sadly, this was not the last time we encountered attitudes like this. It seemed that some of our friends and acquaintances thought that now our "all expenses paid holiday" to the Mediterranean had been cut short, it was time for us to settle down and get ourselves "real" jobs. We could see that moving to another country was one thing, but heading off on a wild-goose chase paid for by other people had been pushing things a bit too far.

It certainly wasn't my intention, but I am sure that many of these people were disappointed by our next move. It was not an invitation to rejoin the police force, but an offer made by OM in South Africa to return to the training center where we had received our six-month orientation, this time to serve as leaders. I was happy to accept. After our long stay in Turkey and a few chaotic weeks of sleeping in different beds and on couches in the houses of relatives, it almost felt like coming home when we drove our little car up the red mud road that led to the OM base.

Settling in had by now almost become a routine with us. Petro once again organized our little household; this time with the few items we could call our own on South African soil. Home would be one of the small cottages set aside for the training leaders. With Benjamin on her hip, she took on the task of catering for the monstrous appetites of the students living on base with us. As it was far from the city, it was a relief to be able to let Martin Junior wander off wherever he wanted to in the wide-open spaces surrounding what we now called home. Dozens of enthusiastic babysitters, in the form of missionaries in training, happily followed him as he discovered the unique South African bugs he had not encountered in Turkey. I immediately took up my new role as teacher and coach with great enthusiasm, sharing our real-life experiences on the mission field, and finally using some of my theological training to teach from the Bible.

With our return to South Africa came a dip in our financial support. I guess failed missionaries don't rank too highly in church budgets. Therefore, apart from my regular teaching work, I launched out in search of new supporters to help fund our work, taking meetings and speaking engagements in different churches. I delivered many moving speeches, explaining the need for the training of missionaries and why we were involved in this ministry.

The problem was, even I was finding it difficult to muster up real passion for the work in which we were now involved. I felt as if I was herding sheep all day, when I would rather have been out fighting wolves. It was difficult to generate enthusiasm for work for which I didn't feel a real calling. After only a few short months, I increasingly found myself longing for Turkey again. I missed the people, the landscape, the ministry and the way of life. The tug on my heart was strong, but I didn't dare tell anyone, let alone Petro, who had decided with me that we needed to be in South Africa.

About six months into our time back in South Africa,

I was on an outreach in Durban with the mission trainees. I managed to slip away and off into the sugar-cane fields, where I was able to spend some time alone in thought and in prayer. As I wandered through the tall, green stalks, I tried to assess my feelings about the direction our lives were taking. It was not that I did not like being in South Africa – it was such a blessing to be back with family and friends and on our beautiful home soil again. Yet nothing helped to ease the niggling feeling of discontent in my heart, which surfaced however hard I tried to suppress it.

I stopped in a furrow between rows of the green cane, and felt the warm KwaZulu Natal sun filter through the leaves. My homeland would always have a strong influence in my life, but now that I was so far away from Turkey, I realized just how strongly that nation had gripped my heart as well. Confused, I called out to God: "Lord – I have to go back. I am desperate. Please, make it possible for us."

It was only a few short weeks later that Petro and I were sitting on the porch of our little cottage, watching the sun go down. It was our favorite part of the day, as well as our favorite place for chatting to each other about our experiences during the day.

"You know that the Coetzees will be leaving for Turkey soon," she said quietly, warming her hands around her mug of hot tea. She took a sip and reached out to touch my hand. "They say you have been a real influence on their decision to go there."

I nodded. In public, I had been enthusiastic and encouraging about the very obvious call on this young couple's lives and had spent a great deal of time with them, sharing our experiences and telling them about what they would encounter and experience in their new field of ministry. Deep down, though, I knew I was jealous. I was envious of the fact that the Lord was clearing the way for them to go, while we had given up our chance of working there. Perhaps to compensate for this, I became an even louder advocate for what they were doing.

Petro sat quietly for a few minutes. It was only recently that she had recovered sufficiently from the hurt we experienced in Turkey to feel comfortable enough to talk about it. She cleared her throat and turned to face me.

"You know what? I wish it were us."

Obviously I had missed something and so blurted out, "What?"

"I wish it was us," she said, resolutely. "I wish we were going back to Turkey. I miss being there—"

I began to talk, but she put up her hand to stop me.

"—that's not to say it wasn't hard sometimes. I didn't like it most of the time. And you didn't help things much, either, always leaving me out of things and working on your own private mission."

I didn't dare interrupt her speech again.

"But – and this is a big but, Martin – if God were to call us back to Turkey, I think I would actually be pleased."

God had done it. I knew that I could never have gone back to Turkey again if it were not with the full support of my wife. Yet, here she was, the woman who had felt so uneasy about going in the first place, now encouraging me to take a step of faith and return. The largest barrier between Turkey and us was being lifted without any effort on my part!

Petro interrupted my thoughts, lightly tapped me on the cheek and said, "Martin – you may close your mouth now."

Suddenly, our lives switched gear. We approached the leadership of OM again to ask their blessing for us to return to Turkey. Amazingly, they supported the idea wholeheartedly.

Perhaps they knew as well as I did that training just wasn't my passion. Suddenly, the support for which we had been praying and working over a number of months came flooding in. We were able to cover the necessary expenses to head back to Turkey and even had a team on board who were willing to work alongside us in prayer and encouragement. There was, however, still the difficult matter of breaking the news to our relatives.

My mom, who had become so used to having the grandchildren around, burst into tears when we told her of our intention to go back. Petro and I sat on the couch, not exactly pleased about being the cause of all the upset. My dad shuffled off to get the Kleenex – but was there a hint of a smile playing on his lips?

Dad squeezed down into the seat next to Mom, handed her a Kleenex and wrapped his arm around her. She continued to cry quietly into his sleeve, but he turned to face us.

"We knew this would happen – been expecting it for a while. It's been great having you around and your mom will miss the children terribly—"

Here my mom broke out into fresh sobs again.

"—but we've known from the beginning that God has a calling on your life. I wasn't impressed by your decision to come back at all, but at least you are now headed in the right direction."

We were on the move again – back to Turkey – but this time the difference was that we were in this together.

Instead of heading back to Ankara, we believed that God wanted us to make a fresh start in Turkey. After much prayer, Petro and I felt led to relocate our family to Mersin, a city on the southern coast of Turkey. Just a quick trip by car from Tarsus, the hometown of the apostle Paul, Mersin is a relatively new city and a cultural melting-pot of people from all over the country.

The busy harbor and fishing industry draw people in search of work from the poorer, eastern parts of Turkey. Unlike the rest of the country, people in this region are well known for their liberalism and openness to accept new ideas and customs. This would be a definite advantage for a pair of Western missionaries and their two light-skinned children seeking to build a new home and ministry.

Mersin is also a melting-pot in a more literal sense. Set in the center of the Chukurova (sunken) Plain, the city has an exceedingly hot climate, with summer temperatures sometimes reaching nearly forty degrees and a sticky coastal humidity to match. It is, in fact, so hot in summer that many people migrate for the season, dragging family, tents, beds and kitchen stove down to the beach or high up into the mountains in search of relief from the heat. Impromptu holiday resorts are erected, often having the appearance of something like refugee camps. Multitudes of families live literally on top of one another in these camps, but, since people from this region are warm, friendly and social, it is all considered part of the fun. It happened on a few occasions that our little family would head into the hills looking for a remote spot for a quiet picnic, only to have a Turkish family set their picnic blanket right next to ours, for fear we might become lonely!

Even though we sensed that it was the right decision to base ourselves in Mersin, we did have some very definite qualms about our new living and working arrangements. Perhaps the biggest concern for me came in the form of the short, steely-eyed German named Heinrich who would be our team leader.

Heinrich, and his wife Anneke, had already been working in Mersin for a number of years, primarily trying to plant churches among the local people. My role would be to support them in this work, as well as continuing with my "religious tourism" career as a front for Bible correspondence courses and literature distribution. He had already achieved a measure of success in the region, with a few well-discipled converts already participating in the church, but he needed extra hands on board to try to expand the work.

I had met him previously at national OM gatherings and had always found him to be a particularly aloof, cold, narrow-minded sort of person. We never seemed to agree completely on many important theological issues. I felt very real concern about how I would manage to work with someone so different from me, let alone submit to his leadership. We were convinced, however, that God wanted us in this city and, well, if things didn't work out, maybe God would move Heinrich somewhere else...

Traveling and setting up house were much easier this time around and we managed to find a wonderful four-bedroom apartment in the city. The two boys got right to work, charming the neighbors and making new friends. At five and three years old, *Ağbi* (big brother) and his angelic-looking sidekick inspired cheek-pinching, gifts of candy and piggyback rides wherever we went. Armed with these two weapons of mass cuteness, Petro and I quickly made new acquaintances.

In fact, it was thanks to the two boys that I met an elderly man named Turgut, who would end up having a profound influence on my life.

Each morning, Martin, Benjamin and I would walk to the community kindergarten, passing the many open shop fronts and market stalls where the locals did all their shopping. This was a fascinating place, teeming with people and full of all sorts of interesting sights and delicious smells. The greengrocer's shop always opened early and little carts loaded high with fresh produce straight from the market were on display. The odor drifting from the fish shop next door was not nearly as enticing, but the boys and I enjoyed the sight of the glistening, goggle-eyed seafood staring blankly up at us from its beds of ice. My favorite store, of course, was the bakery, where one could obtain all sorts of Turkish sweets such as *baklava*, and I often had to remove evidence of tasty treats from the boys' faces quickly before they headed into the classroom.

Next to the bakery was Turgut's shop, a hardware store. It was a modern-day Aladdin's cave, long and narrow, with high shelves reaching to the ceiling and a step-ladder which you could use to reach the highest treasures. With his shop crammed full of goods, Turgut would seat himself on a low stool outside the front door and early each morning he began cajoling passers-by to come and search through his wares. He loved my two boys and we would often stop to chat briefly. Enchanted, he would reach out his thumb and forefinger to pinch the boys' cheeks, often still bearing the telltale signs of *baklava*, and wish them a good day. Naturally, they learnt quite quickly to wish him a good morning from at least an arm's length away.

It was quite surprising, then, to find Turgut's storefront closed one morning. The boys visibly relaxed, relieved to be spared their usual morning ordeal. I felt troubled for a moment, but chose not to worry. But again, there was no Turgut to be seen the next day. I wondered if he was perhaps away on a trip, but then wondered why he hadn't mentioned it during one of our daily chats. It was only on the third morning that I really began to suspect that something was wrong and so looked in at the bakery to ask what had happened.

The short, chubby chap behind the counter grinned when he saw me and immediately reached for the tray of fresh *baklava*. When I asked about his neighbor, though, his whole expression changed and he shook his head dejectedly as he delivered the bad news.

"A stroke," he murmured sadly. "Huge and completely unexpected, too. He's in hospital now, but things are not looking good…" His voice trailed off, and he put the tray of sweets away, obviously assuming that my appetite for food had faded just as quickly as his desire to sell his goods.

I quickly made plans to visit Turgut in the local government hospital that afternoon. There, next to his bed, sat Halime, his wife, a careworn-looking older woman, dressed in the typical Turkish style of long skirt, blouse and modest headscarf. I cautiously introduced myself, edging my way into the room to see my friend.

I was shocked at his appearance. He was paralyzed and though having been in bed for only a few days, his lean frame had already lost weight. Unseeing eyes blinked in his face and he mumbled to himself incoherently.

"What happened?" I asked, shaken.

Halime drew a shaky breath, and seemed to shrink as she sat there on the old hospital chair. "He just collapsed over dinner the other night. The doctors say he won't walk, or talk, or eat again. He can't see. I don't even think he can hear me. I want to comfort him, but I can barely keep myself together…" She dissolved into quiet tears, hiding her face in her shawl, and it was all I could do to try to keep my own composure. Turgut's situation seemed so hopeless and I felt there was little I could do to help.

After a time, Halime regained her composure and we sat in silence for a while, before I carefully offered her the only comfort I could think of.

"Halime – have you ever heard of Jesus, the Messiah?"

"Yes," she responded slowly. "I heard about Him on TV but I don't really know anything about Him."

I put my hand into my shirt pocket and carefully pulled out the small New Testament I always carried with me.

"I am a follower of Jesus the Messiah. I read about Him in the Bible and all of the wonderful things He did when He walked the earth. He healed the sick and He raised the dead." I had her attention. Her eyes lifted up eagerly to meet mine. I continued, "I believe that Jesus loves us and wants to help us. Would you mind if I prayed for Turgut and asked God to heal him?"

I always made a point, whenever the opportunity presented itself, of asking to pray for people. In my many years of ministry in Turkey, I was refused only twice. Muslims, in my experience, value prayer immensely, even when offered in the name of Jesus, and they appreciate the kindness of the gesture.

Tears coursed down her tired cheeks again, but this time her face showed a glimmer of hope. "Yes! Please!" she said eagerly.

I prayed for Turgut, simply asking that God would heal him and that He would reveal Himself to Halime and let her experience His love for her. There was no thunder, lightning or goose-bumps. Nothing dramatic happened. I only felt the peaceful assurance that I had done the right thing in my own heart. As I left, Halime was carefully leafing through the New Testament I had given her, her husband still lying on the narrow hospital bed.

A whole week passed before I was able to return to visit Turgut again. I had been out of town, but was eager to see how he was doing. Having navigated my way successfully through the confusing hospital corridors, I was disappointed to find Turgut's bed empty. My first thought was that he had died, and my heart broke for his poor widow, his grown sons and the shop he so lovingly tended. I made my way to the nurses' station to find out what had happened.

Without even looking up, she replied, "He went home."

"But that's impossible!" I gasped. "He was paralyzed, and—"

The nurse's chin whipped up and with a daring tone in her voice, she exclaimed, "Nothing is impossible!"

It was as if God had reached out and rebuked me. Here was I, the mighty Christian missionary, called to bring hope to the Turkish people, without even a seed of faith that Jesus might have taken me at my word and honored my request that He would help a family in need. Dumbfounded, I stumbled out of the hospital and headed back to my neighborhood, inquiring of neighbors along the way where I might find Turgut's house.

He opened the door himself, a slight limp on his left side, but with a huge grin on his face and the familiar sparkle back in his eyes. In front of me stood a man who, only a few short days ago, had been in such a terrible condition, but God had touched him. He eagerly told me how, after I had prayed, his sight had been restored, he began to hear again and he got up to walk around the ward, to the complete amazement of his wife. Both of them were now desperate to hear more about Jesus. I was blessed with a weekly opportunity to go and share Bible studies with the entire family. I was able to personally disciple Turgut and he became a part of our small church fellowship.

This amazing and encouraging experience reminded me once again of just how eager God is to reach out and reveal Himself to Muslim people, if we are only willing to share His love with them. I decided never again to underestimate the power of God.

Of course, we did not encounter this kind of spiritual high every day. We also experienced times of very real disappointment and monotony, when life seemed stuck in a rut, but it was encouraging to have these memories to look back on and remember the faithfulness of God.

Now that we were properly settled in Mersin, I once again faced the challenge of convincing our neighbors and the government that I had a legitimate reason for being there. My religious tourism company, though perhaps not thriving, at least generated a small amount of work for me, even though our sister company in South Africa had since gone bankrupt. Instead of making the great outdoors my office and ducks my colleagues again, I managed to rent a small shop a few hundred meters from our house and here I could at least maintain the appearance of being a genuine businessman. Petro was thrilled that I would be so close to her and even be able to walk back home for lunch during the day. She helped me to set up office equipment, hang tourism posters on the walls and display a nifty signboard in the window to advertise our business.

Soon I found myself absorbed in the work of simply running a business, no matter how unprofitable it was. There were always faxes to be sent, letters to be answered and reports to be written for the government. I was also very serious about the potential of real religious tourism, hoping to bring churches and prayer groups from South Africa to expose them to the spiritual needs in the Muslim world. For me, time was perhaps not money, but it was precious and I always seemed not to have enough of it.

Of course, to the Turks, time is not really an issue. Ever devoted to the principle of relationships, my neighbors very soon began to make a habit of dropping in for a little visit and a chat in my pleasant headquarters. A "little visit" would entail, at least, a cup of Turkish tea, which I would have to prepare freshly on the gas burner I kept on my desk. This would be sipped daintily from tiny teacups. Then, perhaps, a refill.

And another – and so forth. The usual line of conversational salutations would begin: How was my wife? And my children? My parents? Other members of the extended family? How did I find the weather? The hours would quickly tick by as we were thus occupied by seemingly unending pleasantries, my friend doubtless sitting quite comfortably in my spare office chair, tea in hand, while I nervously fidgeted with paperwork and kept trying to hint subtly that it was time for him to move on. Lace curtains across my big, street-front window seemed to hold the solution; I discovered that so long as I sat very still and kept my front door closed, I could look out, but my neighbors could not see in.

Hasan was a very frequent would-be visitor and his attempts to come in and join me would often repeat themselves like an amusing performance. Casually, Hasan would walk by my office and, in search of fellowship, tap on my closed and locked door. Absorbed in my work, I chose not to respond. However, not one to give up easily, he would knock again, more persistently this time, although receiving no response. Now he was really confused, as he was certain he had seen me leave home for work that morning. He would press his face against the window, fogging up the glass, thinking that perhaps I was hiding in there. Of course, he was right. I sat frozen like a corpse at my desk, careful not to make any movement. Once committed to this course of action, I couldn't quit, because then he would be offended and wonder why I hadn't just let him inside in the first place. Therefore, for as long as he would stand out there, nose pressed flat against the window-pane and big worker's hands grubbing up my window, I would sit like a statue, hardly daring to breathe. Eventually he would give up and move on in search of a cup of tea elsewhere. I would let out a deep sigh of relief, happy to return to my work. The question was, however: was it actually my real work?

Over time, God changed my heart in this regard. Why else was I in Turkey, if not for the people? With my Western, task-oriented mind-set, I tended to see people as an interruption, but this was not how Jesus saw them. I began to notice the many times described in the gospels in which Jesus, on His way to an important task the Father had given Him, would stop and be completely available to those needing help, guidance, or perhaps even just someone to talk to. My work was not the emailing, phoning and photocopying which kept the office running. It was being available to the people looking desperately for some kind of personal connection – so desperately, in fact, that they would come searching out a rude, insensitive foreigner in the hope of finding it. As my attitude changed, so did my office. It became something resembling a train station, with people always on their way in or out, perhaps only dropping in for a few moments to sit and chat before continuing with the rest of their day. The office supply most consumed was soon not paper, but tea-leaves. In time, I even had the immeasurable pleasure of seeing Turkish people who had become my friends make a decision to follow Jesus, right there in the "privacy" of my office. My business, if nothing else, became people.

There were certainly many opportunities to reach out to people in the hustle and bustle of big-city Mersin, but it was important to be smart about the way it was done. In most places around Turkey it was still a crime to distribute evangelistic literature openly. Some Christian missionaries around this time were even set up by the media. They would go to meet a person posing as someone interested in the gospel, only to be exposed on TV and deported. Heinrich and I wanted to be bold in our faith, but at the same time needed to protect our ministry and families.

By chance, we managed to discover quite an ingenious way of finding people who were interested in the gospel. We took advantage of an established Bible study correspondence course, which was offered right across Turkey. We placed weekly advertisements for free copies of the New Testament or the *Jesus* film in a few of the major newspapers. Occasionally, the newspapers would be pressured not to place our advertisements and would drop them, but since we were willing to pay a premium rate for a tiny bit of print space, we were usually able to get our advert in somewhere. There would often be several expressions of interest, some more legitimate than others, but we would always mail the requested materials to anyone who had replied to the ad. Those with further interest would go through the material, complete the prescribed assignments and send them back to us to be graded. The course consisted of several modules and a surprising number of people would eagerly complete every section and then request further information.

This was when matters became interesting. We would make personal contact with the interested party and ask important questions such as, "Why are you interested to know more about Jesus?" and "Who do you think Jesus is?" If they responded favorably, we would plan to meet with them personally in a public place.

Mehmet was one such person. An accountant from Tarsus, he had responded with great interest to the materials we had sent him and excitedly agreed to meet us outside a tea garden. On the day of our meeting, I watched him for a few moments before approaching. Tall and with a dark complexion, he seemed nervous as he sipped tea at a small, private table. However, there were no signs indicating that he was planning an ambush. I approached cautiously, yet with a friendly smile on my face, hoping to put him at ease.

I was relieved to discover that Mehmet, married for ten years and with a steady job, wasn't interested in matters such as a foreign passport, a foreign wife or financial incentives. These were sometimes the reasons for many others expressing interest in Christianity. Amusing rumors of Christian missionaries hiding $100 bills in Bibles to try to convince people to convert often did the rounds in Turkey. True or not, it must really have been a temptation to some, as I received many requests over the years for a little gift to make accepting Jesus easier. Naturally, I would always decline.

Unlike these others, Mehmet expressed a real desire to know Jesus. After a few clandestine meetings in cafés, Mehmet invited me to his home, where I would meet him and his wife and talk to them about the Bible. Cesminaz, a kind, courteous woman, was a little concerned about Mehmet's new-found curiosity about Jesus, but would listen interestedly to everything I explained to them, while serving fruit, nuts and biscuits. Occasionally they would invite Petro and me for a meal and we would spend a long evening with them, discussing the questions that they had about Jesus and the Bible.

It was not uncommon for a person from a Muslim background to ask these questions. Often, they would focus on the authority of the Bible. Cesminaz, naturally anxious about her husband being so interested in the New Testament, asked, "Hasn't the *Injil* [New Testament] been changed? I know that we Muslims respect this book as holy, but I have been told that it has been corrupted."

I wanted to answer, but my mouth was too full of almonds, so Petro responded for me. "The *Injil* that you are holding has not been changed, except to translate it into Turkish so that you can understand. We Christians believe that this book is God's word and that everything it says is true. Many people have tried to find inaccuracies and errors in the Bible, but all of them have failed."

Mehmet rubbed his chin thoughtfully. "But I have now read in the *Injil* that Jesus Himself said He was the Son of God. How can it then be true?"

"You Muslims agree with us that Jesus was a holy man, a prophet, and that Mary was His mother," I explained. "You are taught that Jesus was conceived by a virgin; but how can that happen without the help of a miracle? Someone had to be the father of this child, and it wasn't Joseph, or any other man. God made this man, to be His representative on earth. He is His Father."

Mehmet sighed. "It is all so confusing. This is so different to everything I have been taught before and I have so many questions."

"Good!" I responded enthusiastically. "You have been taught that it is wrong to question faith, but God Himself says here in the Bible that we must enquire of Him and search Him out. Ask Jesus to reveal Himself to you if He really is the Son of God, as He says."

It took two years for Mehmet and Cesminaz to come to faith. For them, accepting Jesus was not an instantaneous decision, but rather a gradual defrosting process. Without even realizing it, they had reached a point where their lives were being influenced more by the Bible, other Christians and the Holy Spirit, than their old Muslim ways. Mehmet became a leader in the church and an influential part of our community of faith.

Not all stories ended as well as that of Mehmet and Cesminaz. Many contacts who had expressed interest gave up as soon as they realized I could not promise them a new job, good health or protection against the authorities. Others, sadly, turned round when they faced opposition from family and friends because of their commitment to Jesus. Even after becoming a member of the local church and accepting the gospel wholeheartedly, some people couldn't persevere and would give up.

"Our church has a wide back door," Heinrich would often comment sadly. "And it is a door that we are never quite able to close."

Perhaps because of these disappointments, Petro and I realized that we had developed a habit of forming relationships purely for the sake of sharing the gospel. With so many lost people in Turkey, it was easy to become overwhelmed and feel pressured to accumulate the largest harvest possible. We began to see people as potential "projects", and would pray that God would lead us to those most likely to be receptive to the message of salvation we had to offer them. While there is not necessarily anything wrong with this, many of our relationships became very shallow, hinging on the condition that if the person were interested in Jesus we would remain friends, but otherwise we would quit wasting our time and move on to someone else.

This was not, however, the way we saw God pursuing relationships in the Bible. His unconditional love reaches out to embrace all people, even those with no interest at all in a friendship with His Son. Infinitely patient, He is the prodigal son's father; always watching, always hopeful, but never coercive or with strings attached to His love. Our prayers changed and instead of asking God to show us people who would make a commitment to Him, we pleaded for good friends with whom we could build long-lasting relationships.

Metin and Aysha, our neighbors, were friends like this, even though we became acquainted through something as trivial as a washing machine. The fifteen-year-old front-loading monstrosity had been a hand-me-down from when we first arrived in Turkey and a frustration in our lives since our first attempt at a rinse cycle. Apparently ill equipped to withstand the rigors of the laundry of a family with small sons, it habitually broke down about once a week. Metin, the local Mr Fixit, would be called upon to come and assess the damage, which, naturally, verged on the edge of being disastrous every time. One week it would be seals, which had perished. The next week a hose would burst. On one occasion, the washer somehow managed to electrocute me, from several meters away, while I was busy soaping myself in the shower. Although every week brought a new type of breakdown, Metin and I enjoyed the predictability of a visit, a cup of tea and a chat. When, with a shuddering groan, the washing machine eventually breathed its last, my friendship with the Turkish couple remained as a legacy.

They never, to our knowledge, made a decision to follow Jesus, but they were wonderful, caring friends with whom we could share everything. We knew that we influenced their lives, through the way we disciplined our children, treated one another and spent our money, but we were most surprised to see that God was even using them to teach and influence us. We began to see many of our friends not just as projects we needed to hurry towards completion, but also as blessings to us from God.

My relationship with my team leader, though, felt more like a curse than a blessing at times. Turks I could deal with, but that hard-headed German was often more than I could cope with. I remember on one occasion, during my personal devotional time, having a distinct feeling that God wanted me to go and pray at one of the biggest mosques in the city. As I often experienced God speaking to me in this way, I was encouraged to raise the issue with Heinrich. It didn't seem like such a big deal to me.

"No," he said.

"No?" I repeated in surprise. "What do you mean, 'No'? God *told* me to do it!"

"That's the issue, Martin. I don't think He really told you to do it. I really do not believe God speaks to us in that way."

For me, this was about as close as a Christian could get to blasphemy and I couldn't do much more than blink for a couple of moments. I knew that Heinrich was from a very traditional, conservative church background. We had disagreed on many other, more trivial issues, but this was ridiculous! How could he be standing there denying God's direction in my life, when he himself had heeded "the call" and become a missionary?

"You mean to tell me—" I felt the all-too-familiar anger simmering, "—that you don't believe God speaks to His children? That I have not been hearing Him all my life? Or that I have been listening to some kind of divine echo, instead of the voice of God?"

Infuriatingly calm, Heinrich interjected, "I didn't say I don't believe God speaks to people. I just don't think He speaks outside of the Bible."

I stormed away before saying something I would regret later. For days, the sting of what he had said to me remained. It was not the only issue between us. When Petro and I had been struggling financially, he was appointed to monitor the way we spent our money. Even at church, we disagreed about the way things should be conducted. We felt increasing friction rising between the two of us.

I wish I could say we found an easy solution to all of our struggles. We didn't. For years, we continued to face confrontation, disagreement and tension. Yet, increasingly, we both found that the bond of faith between us became more important than the areas of conflict. We both worked hard to preserve unity. At times, we both got hurt. However, I learnt to find in Heinrich a loyal, committed, upright friend, with some differences in opinion on the side, but a greater mutual agreement on the fundamentals of our faith.

I didn't know it at the time, but it was friends like these that I would really need in the near future.

Chapter 5

"Honestly, Martin, even if the police found out where our church is, I doubt they'd want to face these six flights of stairs any more than we do," Petro jokingly complained, face flushed from heat and the exertion of hauling Benjamin and all of his gear upstairs.

I shook my head ruefully and tried to concentrate on keeping a tight grip on Martin Junior's sweating, slippery hand as we turned the last corner in the stairwell and finally made it to Heinrich's front door. The unbearable summer heat of Mersin had exhausted us, but at least we had this, our weekly church service with the local believers, to energize us again.

"Good thing he managed to get an apartment on the cooler side of the building," I remarked gratefully. I sharply knocked at the door, hoping to be heard above the din of friends happily chatting inside.

"It's open!" someone called and the four of us bustled inside, quickly caught up in the enthusiastic greetings and friendly kisses for which Turkish people are renowned. Heinrich handed me a cologne bottle with a smile.

"Nearly a full house today," he said. "We are just waiting for Hakan and Miriam to arrive by taxi and then we can start."

I rubbed the cologne into my hands, enjoying the cool, refreshing tingle between my fingers. The heavy scent filled the room and I realized that after many years of living in Turkey, I had finally learnt to associate this smell with friendly hospitality, rather than shaving in the bathroom. "Great," I nodded, heading straight for the coffee table and its delicious spread of biscuits and pastries. "That means I have an hour or so to enjoy the snacks!"

Church services in Turkey were always very predictable: never lacking in fervor, but never starting on time, either. I enjoyed the friendly hustle and bustle before the service began, as brothers and sisters in Christ made their way about Heinrich and Anneke's small apartment, cheerfully enquiring about each other's experiences during the past week, and trying to avoid being knocked over by the energetic children racing around the room.

Anneke had furnished the apartment tastefully in typical Turkish style, with low couches against the walls of the room and a few rugs on the bare and wonderfully cool floor tiles. As our last members arrived, we seated ourselves in a wide circle and Petro took all the children into a bedroom to begin her Sunday school lesson. A reverent hush filled the room and we opened the service in prayer, before I strummed a few chords on my guitar by way of introduction and began leading the group in worship. A few voices joined in hesitantly and I couldn't help grinning at Mehmet, trying to join in the singing with his nose studiously buried in the songbook.

Worship through song is a strange concept for Turkish people. Unfamiliar with Christian culture, they don't have any frame of reference for the many traditions and experiences Western Christians associate closely with our faith. Worship, for a person from a Muslim background, means reading complicated, Arabic prayers. This, of course, does not reflect our idea of an expression of love for the Father. For this reason, Heinrich and I tried to keep the church rituals we introduced to the new Turkish believers as simple as possible: heartfelt, straightforward songs of praise in the local language; short, spontaneous times of prayer and clear, meaningful explanations of texts from the Bible.

This was where Heinrich really shone. Perched on the edge of his chair, he would read a portion of Scripture in Turkish to the group and then in basic terms explain what it meant. For most of these believers, it was through the Bible that they first came to know and love Jesus Christ. It was our wish that they would continue building their lives and faith on the word of God.

About once a month, we shared in the sacrament of Holy Communion. One by one, each believer would tear off a piece of the Turkish flatbread and take a sip of the bright-red cherry juice, thinking on the enormous sacrifice that Jesus Christ had made for them. These men and women understood what sacrifice meant. Many of them had been rejected by family and friends for accepting the gospel. Some had been threatened, or even arrested. For them, this sacrament made the love of Jesus, who laid down His life for us, even more of a reality.

They were not perfect, though. While drawn together by the oneness of knowing Christ, our congregants were also no strangers to gossip, slander and jealousy. Much of the typical Turkish distrust often still simmered beneath the friendly surface of relationships between the believers. We spent a great deal of time and effort intentionally building unity and love between the believers, as well as exposing our small congregation to the wider body of Christ.

In summer-time, this meant gathering with believers from

right across Eastern Turkey for a week-long family camp. Many of these Christians came from congregations made up of as few as three or so people. It was therefore most encouraging for them to be in the company of maybe more than a hundred other people sharing the same struggles, joys and faith.

It always gave me great joy witnessing the reactions of these new Christians when meeting other believers. First, the inevitable distrust and fear surfaced. What if the person worshiping next to you was actually a secret informant for the government? Sometimes it took several days before they started relaxing. Frowning and with arms crossed defensively, they preferred to keep to themselves protectively, whispering furtively to more familiar people when discussion was required. Inevitably, though, all resistance melted and by the end of our time together these men and women discovered deeper, more meaningful friendships than they had ever known before. As at any other Turkish gathering, the decibel level would finally lift sky high. Tent windows and door-flaps would be flung open not only to let the breeze in, but also to invite neighbors in. Children darted through the trees, trying not to upset trays full of tasty goodies set out on picnic blankets between laughing adults. We missionaries knew that God was at work in the hearts of His children.

It was at one such summer gathering that I first met Tilmann. My own tent successfully erected, I set about seeing where else I could offer my services, when I came across the lanky German busily setting up his own tent. He returned my enthusiastic greeting with a mumbled hello and a half-veiled, shy smile. It seemed as if his mouth was hiding beneath his droopy moustache. We spent a little while together, I chatting away happily and banging on tent pegs, he preferring to listen and fiddling with tangled ropes. He certainly seemed like an odd fellow, all arms and legs, with a definite intelligent spark in his eyes, but an obvious inability to express himself verbally. His wife Susanne, on the other hand, kept flitting in and out of the tent in a hurry, chattering away non-stop like a wound-up gramophone. Then she hurried off to greet some old friend who had appeared. At one stage, Tilmann looked across at me and gave a knowing wink, as though wanting to share his secret of having found the perfect, complementary life partner.

I learnt that the couple lived in Adana, just an hour's drive from our home, but were working with another mission organization. With relief, I realized that this in all likelihood meant that our paths would not often cross, except at these yearly social gatherings. It's amusing for me now to realize that God already knew the enormous impact this strange man would have on my life in later years. At the time, though, I thought that one unorthodox, difficult German, in the form of my friend Heinrich, was certainly enough for me to deal with.

The relationship between Heinrich and me was improving, though, perhaps because we were finally learning to accept the differences between us and use them to our advantage. Increasingly, instead of seeing my pioneering recklessness as a threat to his long-term, careful planning for the ministry, he started to encourage me to investigate new ventures.

"Look at this!" I practically shouted at him one morning, thrusting a paperback New Testament into his hands. "Cheap, small, and even better, printed right here in Turkey!"

Heinrich thumbed through the thin, delicate pages of the Testament, his eyes scanning the Turkish script, no doubt unconsciously checking for accuracy. "Legal, then?" he asked.

"Absolutely legal," I grinned. We were both well aware that distribution of religious materials in Turkey was against the law only if they were printed outside the country. "And it's in a modern translation too. Some new agency has started printing them, right here in the province. I can get boxes full of them, easily and inexpensively."

"Great. Do it, then," Heinrich said. He handed the Bible back to me. "Get as many as you need. I'm sure it will be easy enough to raise the financial support."

"I don't doubt that," I nodded, distractedly. "Getting the Bibles will be simple enough. I'm just wondering what to do with them afterwards—"

Heinrich broke out in a delighted chuckle. "Quit beating around the bush, Martin! You're not wondering at all – you have it all figured out already, I know. Give it to me straight, then."

Permission to be frank granted, my plans tumbled out in an excited rush. "You know, as well as I do, that most Christians in Turkey have come to faith because of reading the Bible. You also know how difficult it is to get these Bibles into people's hands. The correspondence courses don't reach everyone and leaving Bibles lying around 'by accident' is not nearly strategic enough."

Heinrich laughed again. My "losing" ministry was well known among my co-workers, probably less for its good intentions than for its lack of any measurable success.

"We need to litter Chukurova province with these Bibles – purposefully, of course. Get them into bookshops, libraries and schools. Sell them, give them out for free, whatever – but get them into the homes of Eastern Turkey."

Heinrich was silent for a moment, obviously thinking it all over. Not one to make rash decisions, he let me stand in nervous anticipation for a few moments. Finally, he spoke.

"Do it then, Martin. If this is something you are passionate about," he paused, as if very carefully measuring his next words, "if this is how God is speaking to you—"

I tried very hard not to let my eyebrows shoot to the ceiling.

"—then, by all means, consider yourself free to give this a shot."

It was in this way that Project Chukurova and Kayra Bible Distribution were born in 1998. Still under the banner of OM, but having registered Kayra as a legal business, I was determined to get many copies of the Turkish New Testament into the remote, and religiously conservative, areas of Eastern Turkey.

On my way out of the door on my first official day of operations, Petro kissed me on the cheek and handed me the briefcase full of Bibles I had packed the night before.

"Be careful, Martin, and know we are praying for you," she said.

If ever there was a wife more tolerant of her husband's wild ideas, I'm sure she and Petro would have a thing or two to chat about.

I decided to throw myself into the proverbial deep end and so, on my first morning on the job, boarded a bus and traveled the dusty, winding mountain pass to Mut, a small village in the north-west of the province. The fact that I had no idea where to start made it an easy decision to have breakfast in a small café. I enjoyed the small-town atmosphere as much as the Turkish sourdough bread and the soft goat's-milk cheese. Praying that God would lead me in the right direction, I set off for the local municipal offices after breakfast.

Mr Aslan, the local mayor, seemed pleased to have a foreigner to show around the town's historic sights. He led me to an ancient monastery, built high in the mountains and overlooking the turquoise Goksun River as it wound its lazy way to the Mediterranean. Proudly, he informed me that it was on this very river that King Frederick I, ruler of Germany and leader of the Third Crusade, drowned while bathing. He told the story dramatically, like a well-known family anecdote, and gave the impression that it had been a profound privilege for the monarch to have drowned in such a tranquil place. At any rate, the crusading armies turned back to Europe after this unusual occurrence, and many lives had probably been saved this way.

Having enjoyed his charming hospitality for most of the day, I offered the mayor a Bible as a parting gift when it was time for me to leave. He accepted it reverently, with the same attitude to holy writings for which most genuine Muslims are known. If not a spectacular victory, at least my first attempt at Bible distribution was the beginning of greater things to come, and I resolved to follow up my new contacts in the future.

"You did *what*?" Abdullah screeched when I told him about my experiences. His effeminate voice reached towards the higher octaves on the musical scale at the best of times, but when he got nervous it flew off the charts. "I don't think you understand. The guy is in government, for goodness' sake! You could have been arrested—"

"It was all perfectly legal," I interrupted, trying to calm him.

"—even if it was legal. You could get yourself seriously messed up. When are you going to learn to be a bit more discreet?"

For Abdullah, finding the balance between standing up for his faith and protecting his life was a daily struggle. Having grown up in a Muslim home, but found little of interest to him in Islam, he had from an early age developed an interest in the Christian faith. I had first met him through the Bible correspondence course. As we sat together in the central park of Tarsus, sipping *ayran* (a cooling mixture of water, yoghurt and salt), we launched headlong into a very serious, heartfelt discussion about Jesus. With the innocence of a child, Abdullah soon came to love and follow the Savior. The thin young man with dark, lank hair suffered from a hormonal disorder, which caused him a great deal of difficulty throughout his life. It was through Jesus that he found both acceptance and courage.

Bravely, Abdullah began to serve alongside me in the Bible distribution ministry. His insight and cultural understanding were invaluable. Over time, he began to travel with me to distribution points more often and even helped to run book tables at fêtes and community events. His dedication to seeing the word of God in the hands of his countrymen was beautiful to observe. Even he, though, didn't always appreciate what he considered recklessness on my part.

As the new ministry continued to grow and I began to recognize the enormous potential it had of reaching many people throughout Eastern Turkey, I started to pray for a more reliable form of transport. Up to this point during our time in Turkey, we had never owned a private vehicle and had instead relied on public transport, just like most other ordinary Turks. This arrangement had always suited us well in the past, but was now beginning to take its toll. Carrying quite a few Bibles at a time back and forth across Eastern Turkey aboard crowded buses and taxis, or else in the trunk of an expensive rental vehicle, was definitely not the most efficient way of carrying out our task.

My dream was to purchase a minivan. It would be so practical, as I could fill the van with boxes full of Bibles and visit more than one city at a time. It could also be used to transport believers to and from church easily and help families to attend our regular church camps in the countryside. There was also no doubt that it would make traveling with Petro and our two boisterous boys a lot easier.

Deciding to investigate the possibility of such a purchase, I walked down to a local car dealership to see what was on offer. The salesperson declared that he had the perfect vehicle for me after a few minutes' discussion and handed me the glossy brochure of a Hyundai minivan. I tried my best not to drool all over the paper in my hand. A twelve-seater, with diesel engine, power steering and electric windows, the bus was perhaps the closest I had ever seen to real luxury. It even had double air-conditioning, which would be wonderful in the middle of summer, when the humidity became unbearable. I was sold on the idea of buying it. There was, however, the small issue of the price to be considered. There was no way in which we, given our current financial situation, could afford such an amazing minivan.

Back home, I called a family meeting at our kitchen table. I showed them the brochure and told them that God was leading me to pray seriously about this vehicle. Martin Junior and Benjamin fingered the brochure excitedly and committed themselves to helping us in the project. We stuck the picture up on the fridge as a reminder and each morning for the following months prayed at breakfast that God would provide for us to buy the minivan.

Over time, we shared with prayer supporters our need for a vehicle and offers of help began to trickle in. People were very keen to play a part in contributing to the project and we managed to raise the enormous sum of 70,000 South African rands (10,000 US dollars at the time) in cash. It was more money than I had ever had at one time, but still I knew that it was nowhere near enough to purchase our dream van. I began to wonder if God wasn't perhaps helping me to see that we had to compromise and be content with something a little less plush. I shopped around again, investigating the prices of cheaper vehicles. Eventually I decided on purchasing another bus, which was definitely still spacious, even if it wouldn't serve the other purposes I had dreamt about. The two little boys didn't stop praying eagerly for that picture on the fridge, though. Of course, it was by now covered with sticky fingerprints and torn around the edges from constant handling.

Finally, eager to put an end to the whole saga, I withdrew the cash from the bank and headed down to the dealership to collect my consolation prize. Excited enough, but definitely feeling just a touch disappointed, I explained to the salesperson that I had decided to purchase the minivan of second choice.

"Are you sure about that?" he asked. "The Hyundai is definitely a better deal and a better minivan for… what you have in mind." Strangely, he usually preferred not to dwell too long on my plans to use the van to transport Bibles and Christians.

"I know," I sighed, "but there is no way I can afford it."

"Are you sure? I might just have a deal for you. A man who has just come in wants to sell his Hyundai van. He is in some kind of financial crisis, and is keen to make a quick sale…"

My heart started beating furiously and my feelings fluctuated between hoping that our dream would come true and wondering whether I was just going to be disappointed again. He took the telephone and called the owner, while I nervously paced up and down the showroom, pockets still stuffed with money.

When the owner drove up in his gleaming, gold-and-blue minivan, I did my best not to show the excitement I was feeling, but it was difficult. He showed me the minivan, let me sit in the comfortable driver's seat and feel the rush of cold air on my face as the air-conditioning was turned up high. Getting out of my dream van, I told him exactly what I had to offer him in cash. It was the one and only offer I could put in.

He paused for a moment, eyeing what had obviously also been his one true love, sadly taking in the beauty of that spectacular vehicle.

"Deal," he said.

It was sold just like that and I became the very proud owner of the van. I gave him the cash and he gently slipped the keys into my hand. With a whoop of joy, I took off down the street in the first vehicle we owned in Turkey and definitely the most lavish one we had ever owned.

Even the sound of the horn was amazing, as Petro and the boys discovered when I pulled into our driveway a few minutes later. They got into and walked around the van, making all the appropriate sounds and demonstrating their admiration with eager squeals while bouncing up and down. Suddenly, Benjamin rushed back into the house, and returned just a moment later with the much doted-on picture from our fridge. The two vehicles were identical, with exactly the same specifications, right down to the gleaming silver mag wheels and gold paintwork we had so fervently admired.

I learnt a truly valuable lesson about being specific when praying that the Lord would provide for our needs and trusting Him to do so. With great thanksgiving, the De Lange family rejoiced that evening, as well as every time we set out on the road, knowing that it was only because of the Lord's faithfulness that we had been so blessed. He truly is a God who wishes to give us the desires of our heart, especially since He is also the One who often puts those desires there in the first place.

In the meantime, it seemed God had been busy placing an altogether different desire in Petro's heart. One evening, she sat doing her embroidery in the soft, muted glow of a table lamp.

I had intended to relax with a good novel that evening, but had put it aside as I distractedly watched my beautiful wife. She had always enjoyed handiwork and I thought that she had never before seemed so lovely as she did now, her hair swept away from her forehead and green eyes intent on her work.

Crafty woman; she always knew how to take advantage of me when I was at my weakest.

Sensing my interest, she looked up to meet my eyes and we shared a smile for a few moments. Leaning across to where I was seated, she spoke softly.

"Honey, may I ask you something?"

"Of course, sweetie. I'm listening."

I knew something was up, but always enjoyed romantic moments like these.

"I've been wondering… how would you feel about having another baby?"

Like a car crash on a cold, wet night, her request hit me with surprising ferocity. Memories of her first two pregnancies tore at the serene atmosphere I had been enjoying so much. I remembered tears, moodiness and midnight runs to the grocery store in search of something, *anything*, to still the desperate cravings of my pregnant wife. Frantically, I tried to come up with a diplomatic response to such a bizarre request.

"Are you sure? You remember what happened at Benjamin's birth…"

"Yes, Martin. I do, but…" She checked herself, and shook her head. "Benjamin is such a blessing. It was a terrible experience, but I feel ready for another child." Moving over to sit against me and putting her head on my shoulder, she went for the kill. "What do you think?"

She, the wiliest of women, had tricked me into a corner as easily as batting her eyes. I desperately turned to my last resort,

Top: The first beginnings of a church in Mersin.

Above: The church building in Mersin.

Right: Turgut in his hardware shop.

Samuel taking a bath.
Our famous washing
machine also features in
the photo.

Above: Martin, the boys and the
much prayed for minivan.

Left: Martin and Stephan at a book
table in Mersin.

Petro and Keiko wrapping Bibles in Mersin.

The leadership of the Mersin church praying for us during our farewell, 27 April 2003.

Martin and Heinrich after the farewell in Mersin, 27 April 2003.

We never did learn to pack light! Our big move to Malatya.

Petro's mom visiting us in Turkey.

The church planting team in Malatya in 2006. Front, left to right, Tilman, Martin and Samuel, and Necati. Back, left to right, Angus, Elizabeth, Susanne, Petro and Semsa.

A team building retreat at Lake Hazar. From left to right: Martin, Tilman, Angus and Necati.

Hussein and Levent.

Martin and Tilman.

Kudret, Ali and his sister.

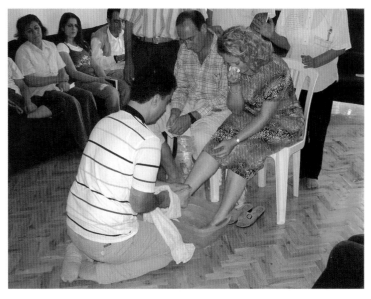

Hussein washes our feet during our farewell service in Malatya, 2006.

Ugur with his fiancée, Nurcan.

The makeshift graves at the memorial ceremony in Pretoria.

Martin in action during a missions presentation in South Africa, 2008.

the same one Christians all over the world use when they can't say no, but don't want to say yes, either.

"May I pray about it?"

"Sure. Just don't take too long."

So I prayed, and God, in His own wonderful way, answered.

Months later, as I lay in bed next to Petro, I could feel her stomach twitching with the subtle kicks of our third son. I contemplated the wonder of God stitching this little one together in his mother's womb, and already knowing him by name. It was, however, on the issue of naming the baby that God and I were in disagreement.

I had woken from a deep sleep that morning, clearly hearing: "Call the boy Samuel."

While always learning, I had come to recognize the sound of the Lord's voice, and this definitely sounded like Him. "Call him Samuel."

The problem was, I did not like the name Samuel. It was an old-fashioned, heavy name, certainly not one with which I would like to burden any son of mine. The gentle nagging of conviction eased as I consoled myself with the idea that, nice as it was for God to help with suggestions, I had the situation firmly under my own control.

At that moment, the ringing of the telephone interrupted my thoughts. Startled, I recalled the last time we had received a phone call so early in the morning. Dad had suffered a heart attack and Mom, barely able to keep it all together, had phoned from the hospital to ask us to pray. Cold fingers of dread gripped me and I raced out to the hallway to pick up the handset.

"Good morning, dear! Are you well?"

Mom certainly sounded chirpy enough.

"Mom? I'm fine. Do you know what time it is…?"

She laughed gaily into my ear. "Oh, no. Have I gotten the time mixed up again? So sorry to wake you. It's just that I have something quite important to tell you. How's Petro?"

"She's doing fine, Mom, and the baby too. So are Martin and Benjamin. You have something important to tell me?"

"Right. As I was praying this morning, I felt that God wanted to give you a message. He wants you to call the boy Samuel."

The pause at my end of the phone was as pregnant as my wife.

"Martin? Are you still there?" I heard my dad in the background asking about a bad connection.

"I'm here, but, Mom – Samuel? I don't want to call him Samuel!" After years of disuse, my boyish whine made an involuntary comeback, just for my mother.

"Well, dear, it's your choice. Don't blame me, I'm just the messenger!" She laughed again, clearly delighted by the whole fiasco, and with an airy "Love to all of you! Have a good day!" she hung up on me.

It was still dark outside and our small wood-burning stove had long ago given its last faint glow of warmth. I hurried back to our warm bed and lay awake next to Petro for a few more hours, silently feeling very confused and sorry for myself.

My confusion didn't abate when the sun rose, either. I didn't get any closer to an answer as Petro's belly continued to swell, her ankles disappeared and our newest addition to the family prepared to make his appearance. In fact, it was just the day before her scheduled C-section, as we sat in my small office drinking tea, that Petro's well of patience dried up and she demanded, in the way that only pregnant women can, that I grow up, be a man and make a decision.

Feeling the need to be methodical about the matter, I

suggested we write names on slips of paper and draw them from a hat.

"You're telling me you want to cast lots to choose a name for our son?" she said, her voice dripping with amused derision.

"It's biblical, isn't it? Look, you take these slips of paper and I'll take some too. Write down the names you like best and we'll pop them into a box." I dug under my desk for a moment, realized that Abdullah had used the last of our boxes for the shipping of Bibles, then grabbed the empty waste-bin instead. Petro rolled her eyes.

"A bin will work fine. You can draw out a slip and the name on it will be the one we use," I declared.

"You promise? This would all have been a lot easier if you had just listened in the first place…"

"Write the names, Petro."

I leaned over my table and wrote out a selection of names that ranked highly on my list: Daniel, David, Nathan and Joshua. Not wanting to be completely disobedient, I even wrote *Samuel* on a slip of paper. I dropped my names into the bin and waited while Petro finished writing hers.

Still feeling the need to maintain a degree of faith in this whole business somehow, I leaned across the table to take Petro's hands, and prayed.

"Father, please help us at this moment. Our boy will be born tomorrow and we really do not know what to name him."

Petro snorted. I continued.

"Help us now to choose the name that You would like him to have. You know how important a name is and what it communicates about a person. Please guide us. In the name of Jesus we pray."

"Amen," Petro said, and reached into the waste-bin.

I held my breath. Petro read the slip of paper and smiled triumphantly. She turned it around for me to see, and my jaw fell open. For on the slip was written *Samuel*.

Just as in the story of young Samuel in the temple, God had spoken and His servant finally decided to listen.

Chapter 6

Samuel, just a few weeks old, lay quietly cooing in his grandmother's arms while Petro hurried about, trying to finish packing the last items.

"I'm really sorry, but I don't think I'll be able to come," she gushed. "There's just too much to be sorted out before we leave. I thought going to the market with a baby was difficult enough, but try preparing for a plane trip!"

It was May 1999 and after several years of living in Turkey, we were finally heading back home to South Africa for a few months of well-deserved rest, reflection and reconnection with family and friends. Petro's mom had kindly flown in to help with the baby and all of our last-minute preparations.

"It's no problem," I soothed. "I'm sure everyone will understand. You stay here and get organized and I'll take Martin and Benjamin to church with me. We might be a while, though."

"Good!" Petro shouted, her head stuck deep into the hall closet. "More time for me to run around without worrying about treading on little toes." She resurfaced, took hold of Martin Junior to smooth some stray hairs, kissed Benjamin on the head and shoved me out of the front door. "Have fun!"

Our little congregation had grown from only a few faithful members to more than thirty and we now met for our Sunday gatherings at my office in downtown Mersin. This particular Sunday, the day before we were due to leave for South Africa, our friends had planned a special goodbye service for us, complete with a fellowship meal afterwards. I expected a gastronomic Turkish spread of epic proportions and had been excited about the event for the last few weeks.

As I began to lead the group in worship that morning, Martin and Benjamin seated beside me, I couldn't help but reflect on how far we had come in just three years. As a family, we had overcome tremendous odds, struggling to adjust to a new culture and life in the ministry. We had come close to quitting, but God had pulled us through. I was so proud of my family, the strength and faithfulness of my wife and the blessing of our three boys. They had all sacrificed so much, but when I looked around the room at the Turkish believers singing with me, I knew that everything we had given up had been worth the effort.

Suddenly, a tremendous banging at the door interrupted our reverent worship. We had just a moment to glance at one another in stunned silence before the door burst open and the room was filled with police officers. There was immediate chaos. Our friends, terrified, leapt to their feet, trying to escape. Big men in blue uniforms darted about, shouting and seizing people, forcibly restraining them against the walls and applying handcuffs. Somewhere in the melee, Heinrich managed to grab hold of Martin Junior and Benjamin and slip discreetly through a side door. The rest of us were hauled out to a police van in front of the building.

"You can't just arrest people!" I complained agitatedly to the officer who seemed to be in charge. In Turkey, gentle reasoning gets you nowhere; success in conflict is directly related to the level of volume applied. I increased my effort. "This is a breach of our constitutional rights! We haven't even been charged."

"Pipe down," he snarled, shoving me into the van. The sweaty smell of fear filled the small space and one or two of the women cried quietly. We had very real reasons to be afraid; police brutality against religious and cultural minorities in Turkey is well documented. Whispered rumors about abuse and torture in custody are common. In addition, Christians who have been arrested face the prospect of being exposed and becoming targets of threats and discrimination in their communities. While all of these realities are things that Turkish believers must learn to accept and expect, it doesn't diminish the danger and fear experienced when it really happens.

We were taken to the central police station and led to a holding cell. Locked inside, and still with no explanation for our arrest, we sat on the hard benches and prayed quietly with one another. The men in particular put on brave faces, but we all knew we were facing a very real and very bad situation.

Meanwhile, safely at home with the boys, Petro had managed not only to notify the members of our prayer chain in South Africa, but also to get hold of the South African embassy and the local consul to intervene on our behalf. He arrived at the police station late that night. He was a big, bald-headed Turk with a successful tourism business and seemed to have the necessary influence – and volume – to ensure that his wishes were granted. Within minutes of his arrival, he strode up to the bars of the cell, a key-wielding constable in his wake, and notified me that I was free to leave. The constable looked a little disappointed that he not only had to let me go, but that this intruder had usurped his right to make such a dramatic announcement.

Relieved, I walked to the door of the cell, thankful that the fiasco was over and our family trip to South Africa was back on the cards. It was only as I turned to say goodbye to my brothers and sisters that my conscience was pricked. No matter the circumstances, it didn't seem right to leave my small congregation to fend for themselves. Some of these men and women I had myself led to Christ and discipled. How could I ask them to take up their crosses and follow Jesus when I was unwilling to do the same?

I placed my hands firmly around the bars of the cell and spoke loudly enough that the police officers could hear too. "I'm afraid I can't go unless everybody else is released as well."

For a moment, the slightest trace of a smile played on Mr Baldy's lips. Very quickly, though, his expression turned serious. "You understand that it might take days for them to charge you? And when they do, they might be able to make these charges stick?"

I nodded.

"Mr De Lange, I hope you realize what a serious situation this is. I cannot guarantee that I will be able to arrange for your release like this again, should you change your mind."

"I won't change my mind," I said. "I will not leave until the same courtesy is offered to the rest of the people in this cell."

"Fair enough," he shrugged, and left to go and talk to the station commander again.

A number of believers reached out to embrace me as I returned to my seat. "Do you know what you are doing?" Nejdet asked.

"No," I replied with half a grin, settling down to try as best I could to make myself comfortable.

It was a long night. Aside from the physical discomfort of

there being so many people crammed into the tiny cell, I am sure we all faced the mental anguish of being anxious about our families and unsure about the future. I worried about the huge costs we had incurred for a family of five to fly halfway across the world and the fact that we might now lose all the money. I was also concerned about how this experience might affect the commitment of the believers who had been arrested with me. For their part, despite their very natural concerns, they seemed to be handling the situation quite well, offering comfort to one another and praying intermittently through the dark midnight hours.

At about nine in the morning, the young constable was at our door again and this time it was his turn to be the bearer of, to him at least, grave tidings. "The charges have all been dropped," he said. "You are free to go."

A shout of joy went up in the cell and as with any Turkish celebration, there were many hugs and kisses to go around. The door was unlocked, and we were set free onto the streets of downtown Mersin. Petro was waiting in front of the police station, our suitcases piled high in the back of the taxi and the children strapped in. The taxi driver had an amused expression on his face. "You like to cut it close, huh?" she grinned, kissing me affectionately on the cheek. "Now, get in, and let's go."

We made it to the airport just in time.

Back in South Africa, we were given a hero's welcome and offered many opportunities to come and share something about our work in Turkey. The fact that I had just faced arrest and imprisonment in a Muslim country seemed to play in my favor, and many churches were excited to hear about our experiences and become involved in some way.

We traveled around South Africa and attended huge churches set in beautifully tended gardens and with row upon row of gleaming, polished wooden pews. It was hard not to compare the huge church buildings, which were often filled to capacity, to our small, intimate church meetings in Turkey.

Usually, we were ushered up to the front row of the church as guests of honor, and Petro would give little Martin and Benjamin a stern look to remind them that everyone could see them and they had better be on their best behavior. It was tough for them to be "on display" for months at a time, but they coped well. After a few hymns, very different in style from what we had become used to, the pastor would invite me to the stage to speak.

Not one to let an opportunity for some fun and drama pass by, I immensely enjoyed walking to meet the pastor with dignity, but instead of accepting his outstretched hand for a polite handshake, I would grasp his shoulders and proceed to kiss him on both cheeks in the Turkish fashion of greeting. The manly man's face would often flush in sudden horror, sometimes prompting me to repeat the performance considered very respectful in Turkey. The amused congregation, of course, would burst into peals of delighted laughter at their pastor's profound embarrassment.

Recovering, the pastor might need a moment to straighten his tie and clear his throat, but usually had enough courage to respond, "Er, thank you, Martin, for that… cultural experience. We look forward to hearing more about your time in Turkey," before gratefully handing over to me. It was always an amusing way to begin a service, but I did it intentionally, knowing that much of what I had to share would be not nearly so light or humorous.

As done during many other presentations by missionaries, I would share pictures of Turkey and information about some of our friends living there. Many of the people in the churches really had no idea what Turkey was like and had possibly never even met a Muslim person. It was therefore exciting to be able to demystify the country and its people. Up to this point of my presentation, people were probably quite enjoying it and interested in what I had to show them. Then, however, I would reach the crux of the matter.

Opening my Bible, I would read Luke 10:1–3:

> *After this the Lord appointed seventy-two others and sent them two by two ahead of him to every town and place where he was about to go. He told them, "The harvest is plentiful, but the workers are few. Ask the Lord of the harvest, therefore, to send out workers into his harvest field. Go! I am sending you out like lambs among wolves."*

"The problems we are facing in world evangelism are not with the harvest," I would declare. "Jesus Himself said that the harvest is plentiful. I have seen in Turkey just some of the millions and millions of people who are desperate to hear about Jesus. The Holy Spirit is always busy preparing hearts to know God.

"The main problem lies, according to Jesus, with the workers who must bring in the harvest. There are not enough of them! In Turkey, there are more than 70 million people. Less than half a per cent of them are Christians. Many have never even heard about Jesus. Yet there are only a few hundred Christian missionaries ministering to those millions of people!

"Throughout the Muslim world, there are about 300,000 non-Christians for every Christian missionary working in the fields. Such a large harvest, but so few people to bring it in! We must pray God would send out more missionaries into the field."

I could see many heads nodding in the crowd and while the numbers sometimes shocked people, there was not much for them to disagree with – yet.

"Jesus goes on to tell us how He sends these workers out: like lambs among wolves. Lambs are not particularly smart or strong creatures. They are just weak young animals. They have no natural defenses. A lamb among wolves is going to be eaten, no doubt about it. He is going to pay with his life. As someone sent out by Jesus, a harvester goes with the same understanding as that lamb – he may have to sacrifice his life for the sake of the gospel.

"So, there are not enough of these harvesters and the ones who do go are putting their comfort, finances, opportunities, safety and even lives on the line. When Jesus then says He is sending people out to be harvesters, whom is He talking about?"

By now, the congregation would be squirming in their seats. They knew the answer, but would prefer not to have to admit it out loud.

"We are the harvesters, people! All of us are sent by God to go out and make disciples. In Matthew 28, Jesus shares His last words with His disciples. His last words must have been very important, something Jesus wanted His people to remember before He left them to return to heaven. This is what He said: 'Go out to all the nations and make disciples of them.' This is a command, a commission, to all God's people. We must all obey and become part of it.

"I find it amazing that people can tell me, 'I am not meant to be a missionary – God has not told me to go.' Do they not read their Bibles? Or are their Bibles different from mine? Because in my Bible Jesus says clearly that we, His disciples, are all called to go. Rather, ask God to show you clearly if you are meant to stay!

"My family and I have paid a high price for following Jesus. I know many others who have sacrificed even more. However, in view of what Jesus did for me, I would say that it has definitely been worth it. Are you willing to be obedient and answer the call for more workers in the field?"

Silence would descend on the church. I never intended this to be a simple question, but rather a challenge, not to be taken lightly. As I began preparing to leave the stage, I asked that anyone who was willing to commit to serving God in this mission should stand in a public declaration of obedience. Sometimes we would wait quietly for a few minutes before one or two young people might stand. Occasionally, they would be left standing alone, far fewer people than there needed to be. Often, inspired by the bravery of the first few individuals, large numbers of the congregation would rise to their feet as an outward sign of an internal promise. We would pray together, trusting the Holy Spirit to see the true attitudes of people's hearts. Even still, I couldn't help but feel a little disappointed that there were not nearly enough people willing to respond positively to what they had read in God's word.

Being separated from my friends and life in Turkey for months at a time was never easy for me. Despite the comfort of being in a Christian country, where I could be open about my faith, I desperately missed the deep fellowship I shared with the other believers in Turkey. I missed their commitment to the faith which developed from the suffering and persecution they experienced. This was something almost unknown to the church in South Africa. My children missed their friends, the Turkish language and the food with which they had grown up. Petro missed the crowded, busy market-places where she would bargain for our daily groceries. As wonderful as furlough was, it sometimes made us appreciate even more just how attached to life in Turkey we had become.

In August 1999, a few weeks before we were due to return to Turkey, we were given the opportunity to stay in a very fancy hotel near the beach in Port Elizabeth for a few nights. We were treated like royalty; Petro didn't have to do any cooking for a few days and enjoyed her time with little Samuel, while the bigger boys and I ran about on the breezy beach every morning.

Early one morning, I set out for a brisk jog along the seafront. It was a different kind of seaside from the one in Turkey. It was not nearly as warm or balmy, but pleasant in its own way. The physical exertion helped me to clear my head of the tiredness brought on by weeks of meetings and talks across the country. As I panted back along the path to our hotel, I enjoyed thinking about the fact that we would be returning soon.

I crashed through the front door, and leaned against the large sofa for a few minutes to catch my breath, before realizing that everybody else was still asleep. Tiptoeing to the kitchen, I helped myself to a large gulp of water from the fridge and flopped down onto the couch to catch a few minutes of the news on TV.

When Petro woke up and emerged from the bedroom, she found me sitting bolt upright, my face stricken and eyes glued to the television screen. An earthquake, registering seven on the Richter scale, had hit Istanbul, leaving 20,000 people dead, others trapped alive and the city in complete chaos. The images were horrific. Whole apartment blocks had been reduced to piles of concrete and twisted metal bars, and the normally bustling city streets of Istanbul were filled with debris. Dazed people could be seen wandering through all of this, some calling out hoarsely for loved ones, others just observing the destruction through red-rimmed eyes peering out of their grimy faces. I wept quietly on the sofa, imagining the grief that my adopted countrymen must have been experiencing and wishing desperately that I could have been there to offer some form of help.

Arriving in Turkey just a few days later, we quickly joined a relief team finding temporary accommodation for people who had lost their homes in the earthquake. In some villages, the people possessed nothing but the pajamas in which they had fled their houses on the night of the quakes. The relief and development branch of our organization assembled tents, supplied clean drinking water and offered emotional support during those first terrible weeks after the disaster. I carried the shocking images and stories back home to Mersin with me, shaken by how quickly so much could be lost and appreciating my loved ones and friends more than ever before.

Some months later, feeling the last rays of summer sunshine on my shoulders, I was enjoying a stroll home from my office, reflecting on the many promising conversations and tasty cups of tea I had enjoyed with visitors during the day. Strengthened by faith, I could clearly see how each chat, each chance encounter, with the people God had placed along my way, was leading them closer to a clearer understanding of the message of the gospel. Filled with hope for the future, I was reminded yet again of God's relentless efforts in drawing people to Him.

When I was about 200 meters from our front door, the early evening was suddenly filled with a brief, eerie silence. Then, with frightening speed, an ominous rumble tore through the stillness and rushed towards me. In front of me, I saw the road begin to sway and pitch, as though it had suddenly become a black, tarred sea. Rows of buildings by the side of the road, which before had looked so strong and immovable, were torn apart and danced about to the sounds of a strange cracking, creaking symphony. For a few moments, I struggled just to maintain my footing. Then, with great shock, I realized that my whole family, the people most precious to me in the whole world, was just a few paces away from me in one of the disintegrating apartment blocks. I was caught up in the middle of an earthquake and, worse still, so was my family.

The images I had seen on television just months earlier reeled through my mind. I willed my feet to move and took off towards our home at a sprint, yelling out the names of my wife and children with astonishing ferocity. A distance which before had seemed like a short walk now dragged on for eternity as I lunged down the pavement, my cries drowned by the continuing growl of the earthquake and shouts of terrified people on the street.

As I neared our front door, I almost ran into Petro, who was streaking down the stairs like a flash, children hot on her heels. Relieved, I threw an ashen-faced Benjamin under one of my arms, grabbed hold of Martin and ushered my family out into an open area of the street.

Just as suddenly as it began, the tremor stopped. A heavy silence descended upon our street, broken only occasionally by the sound of a piece of masonry falling from a building to the street below. In shocked solidarity, neighbors quickly banded together to search for missing family members amid the rubble. Thankfully, nobody had been killed, but the oppressive fear that struck at our hearts was very deep and strong.

We spent that night just like all the other people in our community – out in the street, too afraid to go back home. Very few of us slept as we sat about in small hushed circles on the ground, the adrenaline pumping in our veins keeping us much too busy listening for the first signs of an aftershock to be very interested in conversation. I was overwhelmed by deep love and appreciation for my family and thanked God for keeping them safe.

Even when we were able to return home and when I had a pillow instead of a curb on which to rest my head, it proved difficult to sleep at night. The sights, sounds and deep fear I had felt for my family would return as soon as I closed my eyes, and I went to bed at night with the knowledge that everything I valued and everyone I loved might be taken from me in just a moment. I was haunted, not so much by the idea of dying, as by the possibility of being trapped alive under tons of rubble, not knowing what had happened to my family and when, if at all, someone would come to rescue us. Petro only had to roll over in bed at night for me to be up and ready to evacuate everybody. The stress began to wear me out emotionally and I certainly didn't win much love from my wife by comparing her movements to a seismic shift in the crust of the earth.

It took time, but I came to realize through studying the Scriptures that the fear I was experiencing was not from God, but was a weapon of oppression used by the evil one. Jesus clearly states that He came to bring us peace from God, yet I had allowed a frantic, all-consuming terror to overcome me. Through the help of the Holy Spirit, I learnt to rebuke my fear and command it to leave me and to accept the peace which surpasses all understanding offered by God.

This experience reminded me again, though, of the temporary nature of our lives on this earth. In just a twinkling of an eye, I might be taken to live with Jesus forever. It could happen amid the booming thunder of an earthquake, at the hand of a Muslim fanatic, or even peacefully, unexpectedly, in my sleep. I was empowered by this knowledge and resolved to treat the fear of rejection I experienced when witnessing to my neighbors, or the fear of imprisonment when distributing Bibles, in the same way as I had dealt with my fears related to the earthquake. I knew that God was in control and accepted His kingship in my life. Over the following years, as the risks of our presence in Turkey intensified, I increasingly had to ask God to remind me of this truth.

One day, the jingling bell at the door of my office alerted me to a visitor arriving to greet me and share a cup of tea. I was happy enough to see him, but knew quite quickly that for him this was not a social call – it was business. I had spent enough time working with the long arm of the law in South Africa to be able to detect a police officer a mile away. He had been there several times before, claiming to be interested in Christianity and the Bible, but obviously much keener on getting a glimpse of some of the illicit secrets I might be hiding in my small, modestly furnished workplace.

Feigning ignorance, I poured him a drink and settled down for a pleasant, friendly interchange. "How is your wife?" I enquired cheerfully. "Your father? Your mother? How have you been experiencing the weather?"

Part of me knew that he needed the Savior as much as anybody else needed Him, and hoped to have a meaningful conversation about this with him. The other part of me, however, enjoyed the idea of leading him on at his own game.

He answered with a non-committal grunt, his eyes roaming my desk for a piece of incriminating evidence. We sat in silence for a few minutes, I happily grinning and trying to cool my steaming tea, while he appeared to become significantly less comfortable with the arrangement. Finally, he decided to take the plunge, asking the question he'd been dying to ask: "Don't you have a Bible for me?"

"A Bible?" I asked, raising my eyebrow in surprise. "That's an interesting request. You know, handing Bibles out here is enough to get a person into trouble. Of course, you and I also know that there is nothing actually illegal about doing so."

I always quite seriously made it my personal mission to re-educate the Turkish police about constitutional rights, relishing the opportunity to set them right.

I continued, "If you really wanted a Bible, though, maybe I could manage to get a hold of one for you. Say! I could drop it off at your precinct this afternoon – I'll be there to collect our residency permits. You're at the central police station, right?"

His face turned as red as the Turkish flag and he nearly dropped his teacup in his haste to get up and out of my office as quickly as possible. Perhaps if he had realized that I had been trained to be every bit as observant as he was, he would have been a bit more cautious about showing his face when I made my regular treks downtown to file the paperwork for our visas.

The Turkish police seemed to take great pleasure in helping – or more often hindering – me in my quest to remain a legal visitor to their country. I had to face long hours of filing forms and standing in queues to ensure that each member of the De Lange family was in possession of the necessary documents and signatures to guarantee our continued presence in Mersin. It was a real hassle, but I certainly didn't want to jeopardize the ministry by putting a foot wrong.

On this particular occasion, months of filing applications had finally warranted a renewal of our residency permits and I had been summoned to police headquarters to collect them. I sat and waited in a plastic chair in the large office of the policeman in charge, while he scanned my file on the desk in front of him, a serious expression on his face. Appearing to be satisfied, he stood up to go and retrieve our permits from the filing cabinet behind him and, like a good detective, I used the opportunity to sneak a peek at the file on his desk.

My name was printed severely in bold capital letters along the margin of the folder and I was surprised to see how thick the file was. Quickly and quietly, I paged through papers filled with writing; dates and endless notes had been recorded there. Even more surprising to me were the documents headed by the big red letters of a government stamp. The stamp read, "Top Secret".

Mind reeling, I slid back into my seat as the policeman found what he had been looking for and turned to hand the permits to me. I was stunned that so much time and effort had been put into tracking my movements and finding out information about me. Exactly what did they think they had on me that warranted a *top-secret* file?

As time progressed, I became more and more aware that my movements and relationships were being monitored. They were always there, following me with their eyes from where they were seated on the back seat of the bus in which I traveled, or peeking out from behind the tinted windows of the unmarked Renault sedans in which they followed me. I even got the impression that my telephone conversations were being tapped. This was not the deluded paranoia of someone mentally unbalanced; there was real evidence that the authorities were aware of my presence in the country, and unhappy about the work I was doing.

Recent investigations into police brutality in Turkey have uncovered alleged government-sponsored plans to turn public opinion against non-Muslims, as well as links between the Turkish police and right-wing Muslim extremist groups at the time. Some leaked documents have gone so far as to suggest that the government and certain sections of the police department openly supported violence towards and persecution of Christians and Christian workers in Turkey. I couldn't have known it at the time, but the attitudes of police towards my family and me were evidence of a growing hatred of Christian missionary activity, which would surface in disastrous ways in the coming years.

While not privy to the heated conversations and secret briefings going on in government offices throughout Turkey at the time, I certainly remained aware of the risks I faced in ministry. Despite this, I chose to remain faithful to the calling that God had placed on our family, every day becoming more aware of the need to surrender my fears to God.

Meanwhile, we were able to increase Bible distribution throughout the Chukurova province. Abdullah and I had stumbled onto a particularly effective way of getting Bibles into people's hands, using local bookstores as our main distribution points. Heinrich had constructed a number of easily assembled bookshelves for us. We offered these to booksellers to display our products. We took on the responsibility of providing the Bibles for the shelves and restocking them when necessary and agreed to share part of the profits of book sales with the store. It was a win–win situation for everybody. Most store managers eagerly agreed to our proposals, despite the occasional harassment they received for displaying religious "propaganda" in their shops. Right from the beginning, we experienced quite a phenomenal turnover, with Bibles and other Christian books flying from the shelves almost as soon as we had put them there.

Always in search of a fresh challenge, I set my sights on the city of Konya as a new distribution point in the east of Turkey. A city devoid of spiritual light, Konya had the highest concentration of mosques in the whole of Turkey, but no local Christian church for its 600,000 inhabitants. A few brave missionaries were based in the city, but they faced enormous challenges in reaching people for Christ. This could perhaps partially be ascribed to the large Muslim theological university, the students of which formed a major part of the community.

Eagerly, Abdullah and I set out on our first trip to the region in 2000, the minivan packed to capacity with Bibles and other Christian literature. Managing to find a parking spot in the city center, we set off towards some of the more popular bookstores to peddle our wares. Surprisingly, many stores were interested. Most agreed to take at least one or two Bibles on a trial basis before committing themselves to taking on more stock. It seemed that they were enthusiastic about becoming more actively involved once the trial run proved to be a success. Occasionally, we encountered a shop owner who was not at all interested and maybe even a little offended that we would suggest the idea, but Abdullah and I had developed thick skins by this stage and we would simply bid the angry man a good day before moving on to the next store.

Our last visit for the day was to a dingy store in the basement of a large shopping center in the middle of town. As we entered the store, we politely greeted the young man, whom we assumed to be the manager, sitting behind his large wooden desk, as well as an older man who had obviously dropped in for a visit. The dignified elderly man rose from his seat, his long white robes hanging to his ankles, their length almost equaled by that of his white beard.

"Mohammed Demir," he introduced himself, with an extended hand and a kiss on our cheeks. "I lecture at the Islamic university. And this is Dursun, one of my students."

Abdullah stiffened next to me and I had to nudge him lightly to remind him to relax. We took our seats in front of the desk and got down to business, explaining our purpose for being in the city and the services we had to offer. While Dursun looked slightly nervous to have these two Christians sitting across from him in his shop, Mr Demir listened to each word we said very carefully, his intelligent eyes beneath their thick, bushy brows taking in everything about us with great intensity.

Usually, I would not engage in debate on theological issues with a Turk. Wanting to understand exactly what Muslim people believe, I have read the Quran a number of times, only to discover that this made me far more knowledgeable about Islamic doctrine than the average person. Many Muslims have never really read the Quran themselves, but are taught to listen to and believe what their Imams teach them. Muslims are taught that faith requires one never to question spiritual matters. Because of this, I discovered that difficult questions, or questions requiring insight, would often shut down a conversation rather than stimulate further thought.

On this occasion, however, I was delighted to have encountered an exciting opportunity for discussion, since the professor would surely have more than just a basic understanding of Islam. Turning to Dursun, I said, "I am a follower of the teachings of Jesus, and you are a Muslim. However, I know there must be some things on which we can agree. Tell me – do you believe that Jesus is a prophet?"

Eager to flex his spiritual muscles, especially in the presence of his teacher, Dursun brightened up immediately at such an easy question and excitedly told me that he believed this to be true. Dursun's mentor also nodded his head slightly, obviously interested in where I intended going with the conversation.

"Ah, so we are of one mind in that respect. Perhaps I may also ask you this: Do you believe that Jesus will come back one day?"

"I do believe that!" Dursun exclaimed. "I have been taught that Jesus will return to this world. Then He will be married, have children and finally die and be buried."

Though I definitely had some different opinions about what Dursun had just said, I confirmed that I also believed in the second coming of Jesus. I turned to the professor and addressed my next question to him.

"Do you believe that a prophet can ever lose his title?"

The professor shook his head. "No, he cannot."

"So, Jesus is, and will always be, a prophet?"

Dursun nodded eagerly, although Mr Demir looked slightly concerned about the turn the conversation was taking. Knowing that Muslims believe all prophets to be without sin and that they cannot ever lose their status as a prophet, I leaned over the table to face Dursun again to present my closing argument.

"So, then, Dursun, if you believe Jesus to be a prophet, a title which can never be taken away from Him, and you believe that Jesus is to return to earth – who is the last prophet?"

Just a faint squeak escaped Dursun's throat as he tried to comprehend the difficult position I had just put him in. His teacher rose quickly to his feet, and cautioned Dursun, "You don't need to answer this blasphemy!"

There was no need for the warning – the implied answer to the question was clear, but Dursun could not possibly admit it, lest he deny the whole basis of his faith. Muslims believe that Mohammed, the last living prophet, was the final authority on matters of faith and that his teachings superseded the principles espoused by previous prophets, including Jesus. Yet if Jesus was in fact the last prophet, His authority overruled that of Mohammed and the whole foundation of the religion of Islam would be lost.

Abdullah, having recovered from his nervousness, did his best to hide the victorious grin on his face as Mr Demir unceremoniously asked us to leave the store, while poor Dursun sat at his desk dejectedly, a puzzled expression on his face. I pitied him for the crisis of faith he was experiencing, but rejoiced in knowing that, by facing such colossal questions, he was perhaps for the first time in his life moving a step closer to the truth.

Experiencing such a spiritual high in Konya buoyed up our spirits and Abdullah and I joyfully continued our journey the following day and drove through the winding mountain passes to our next stop, Urgup, in Cappadocia.

We certainly saw no reason to curb our joy. A region of exquisite natural beauty, Cappadocia also boasts a rich heritage of historical sites. Beautiful cities carved from the rocks, cobblestone streets and labyrinths of underground tunnels used by early Christians to escape Roman persecution all bear testimony to its rich past. Usually, I could not resist stopping in the town, even if just for a quick snack in one of the open-air market-places, full of carpet-sellers and the delicious, wafting smell of brewing coffee.

Perhaps, under different circumstances, we would have been more attuned to the uncanny silence in the streets. Even the presence of two fierce-looking police officers outside of the library did not alarm us, as we hurried inside to donate a few Bibles.

"After this stop, I suspect it is time for some *baklava*," Abdullah grinned, and I nodded with a laugh, coming to a stop before the reception desk in the huge, old lobby.

The secretary, a slim, young Turkish girl, asked our names politely enough, but her fingers trembled just a little when she dialed the manager's telephone extension and then pointed us to his door with hesitation.

It was too late to back out by the time we noticed the two police officers closing the main door of the library behind us, and the plain-clothes detectives standing to attention inside the manager's office. The portly manager, grinning like a hero, had only to stand aside before the detectives leapt at us and snapped handcuffs onto our wrists. Within seconds, an expression of shock and fear replaced the jovial one on Abdullah's face. He was just twenty years old and was not only a Christian, but also a Turkish Christian, in a Muslim state where the police rule. He and I both knew that he, in particular, was in big trouble.

"My dad is going to kill me…" he managed to groan, as we were dragged from the library into a waiting police car.

Down at the police station, I noticed that our minivan had already been seized and was being searched thoroughly by police officers. I sighed inwardly. Inside the minivan were about 1,000 Bibles, as well as all my personal information and documents. If there was anything in our vehicle that could incriminate us, it seemed that the police were very determined to find it.

I barely managed to send off a quick text message to Petro before my cell phone was confiscated. I was briskly patted down before being pushed along a dank, smelly corridor to a holding cell. Abdullah was locked into the cell next to mine with an abrupt clang of the door and I heard him slide down the wall and begin to sob softly.

"We'll be okay," I called out, hoping to comfort him, but knowing that our dark, wet surroundings would do little to inspire much confidence in my claim. "We need to pray, Abdullah. Trust in God."

I wished that I could be closer to him and able to offer a bit more comfort. He was such a young person, who had faced so much trauma and rejection in his life. I could hardly imagine how difficult this situation would be for him now.

The sound of brisk footsteps made its way down the hall and I heard Abdullah's cell door swing open again.

"What is your business with this foreign dog?" an officer yelled.

"He is my boss," I heard Abdullah reply.

The sound of a severe slap reverberated through his cell and Abdullah cried out in alarm and pain as he was repeatedly beaten in the face and on the head. I leapt to my feet and stuck my face as far as I could through the bars of my door, shouting at the officer to stop. My fear, which I had struggled to control since the time of the earthquake, disappeared under the influence of a holy boldness that left me concerned only for the safety of my friend. The abuse continued intermittently for the next few hours and in between I could hear Abdullah weeping alone on the concrete floor. I could only wonder, if this was how they treated the assistant, what they might have in store for me.

Sometime later in the evening, I was finally summoned to an interrogation room. From snatches of conversation I had overheard, I learnt that a certain Chief Officer Osman had especially been brought in from a nearby city to assist in my questioning. He was an imposing character, with deep lines etching his face and a thick frame. Even the other police stood to attention when he strode in.

Refusing to play along with the old trick of police intimidation, I took my seat on the steel chair pointed out to me and crossed my legs nonchalantly.

I was hit with such infuriated force that I was thrown from the chair onto the floor. My initial reaction was to jump to my feet and fight back, but in that moment I was reminded of the words of Jesus: "If someone slaps you on one cheek, turn the other one also." I must admit that my thoughts were not so much concerned with repentance as with wondering why Jesus had to choose this particular method of teaching me about humility.

With my face burning as much from embarrassment as from the tremendous smack I had received, I returned to my seat meekly. Obviously, though, Osman thought that I wasn't meek enough yet. In one fluid movement, he reached out, grabbed me by the shirt and with brute force flung me towards the far corner of the room. I slid across the concrete floor on my back and hit the wall with a thump. In a moment, he was on top of me again, dragging me by the scruff of my neck and throwing me back into my chair. His speed surprised me more than his strength. This clearly was a man used to getting what he wanted out of the suspects he dealt with.

Osman planted his massive palms on my knees and leaned in towards me until his face was just centimeters from my own.

"Who sent you here?" he demanded through clenched, tea-stained teeth.

Before I had a chance to answer, he spat more questions at me: "Who pays you? Where do you get your money?"

If he was trying to rattle me, he was certainly succeeding. I didn't have a chance to gather my thoughts enough to answer any of the barrage of questions being flung at me. I couldn't help thinking that this was perhaps a little bit how I had made Dursun feel earlier in the day. I wanted to give the right answers, but I knew anything I said might be used to trap me. I prayed desperately, asking God to give me wisdom. Finally, I decided just to answer as honestly as I could.

"God sent me," I replied. "And God provides me with everything I need."

This wasn't quite the response that Osman was looking

for and he swooped in again with another quick succession of questions. The police had searched my vehicle, he said, and had found the religious materials. My secret was out and they knew exactly what I was up to.

"I'm not hiding anything," I said. "I'm not doing anything illegal either. You're even welcome to keep the Bibles, if you like."

The interrogation continued through the night, but eventually it must have dawned on them that they weren't going to get anything worthwhile out of me and I was returned to my cell. Exhausted, I fell asleep immediately, with my jacket rolled up to serve as a pillow on the long, steel bench that was my bed.

When we were woken up early the next morning, it was with good news. The state prosecutor had insisted that he would not be able to present a case against us and our docket was thrown out. As suddenly as we had been taken in, Abdullah and I were released under stern orders from the police captain never to return to his city. Abdullah, his face still bruised and puffy after everything he had been through, shared a prayer of thanksgiving with me on the stairs of the police station and then allowed me to lead him out to our ransacked minivan.

We both stopped suddenly when Officer Osman appeared on the footpath in front of us. He looked no less menacing in daylight, but this time it was an apologetic smile on his face instead of a grimace.

"Sorry about that," he murmured, with a quick pat on my shoulder. "Nothing personal, you know."

I got into the driver's seat of our minivan, still a little bit shaken up, but also close to laughing about the unusual ways in which God sorted out our difficult situations.

Abdullah and I were subdued on our drive back home.

Afraid of the reaction of his family when he returned home, Abdullah spent much time praying that God would help him to remain strong, even in the face of opposition. I prayed that the difficult experiences would serve to draw him closer to Jesus and would not prove to be an obstacle in his walk with God.

It was with relief that I finally turned into our street in Mersin. The sun was just beginning its slow descent to the horizon and I found the familiarity of home comforting after such an unusual outing. As I slowly slipped out of my seat and closed the door behind me, I saw Petro hurrying down the steps towards me and was once again so grateful for her support, knowing that she would have been praying for me since receiving that hasty message the night before. Living in Turkey and being involved in the ministry entailed being at constant risk. This I knew more clearly now than ever before, yet, despite the distressing evening, I still felt confident that I was willing to take these risks for the sake of the gospel and for Turkish believers like Abdullah. I wrapped my wife into a firm embrace, and realized that I couldn't imagine doing ministry in Turkey without the love and care of the wonderful woman in my arms.

Suddenly no longer concerned about what the neighbors thought about public displays of affection, I leaned down to kiss my wife. Petro blushed and tried to remind me how much the Turks love gossip, but at that moment I didn't care.

I probably should have cared just a little more, though. Benjamin was next to burst through the front door and it was with just as little thought of decorum that he shrieked in Turkish, at a volume loud enough to turn heads right to the end of our block, "Daddy, Daddy! I'm so glad you're out of jail!"

Now *that* really gave the neighbors something to gossip about.

Chapter 7

We continued to face opposition from the authorities during our eight years in Mersin. We encountered disappointments and setbacks, sometimes even at the hands of Christians from within our small fellowships. Relationships between missionary team members were at times strained, as were our connections with family and friends back home in South Africa; yet we experienced great blessing and satisfaction living, ministering and growing there on the warm coastline of Turkey.

On a balmy Saturday afternoon in 2002, Petro and I sat enjoying the shade of a creeper that we had faithfully tended over the years. It cast a refreshing, green-tinged shadow across our porch and filled the air with the perfume of its exotic flowers. During the week we were very busy, occupied by inter-city ministry trips and appointments, school commitments for the children and the usual day-to-day tasks involved in running a household. Sundays were equally demanding, with church services sometimes running into the early afternoon. Saturdays, though, remained our time of rest, reserved for simple pleasures and special moments shared between us as a family.

Petro laughed as I shared a story about one of my regular

chats with Hasan in my office during the week.

"You've made good friends here," she reflected. "Many lives have been touched just because you are willing to be gracious with your time."

Nodding, I silently thanked God for His kindness to us. Mersin had been our training ground and God had worked in us as much as He had worked through us during our time there.

"They've touched my life too. I know I have changed a lot in the last few years…"

"Definitely for the better," Petro quipped sagely, and I gave her a light swat on the knee in retribution. She laughed again, and I repositioned myself in my cozy deckchair, enjoying the feeling of Saturday afternoon laziness washing over me.

With eyes half closed, I reflected meditatively, "Yes, they have really been good years…"

Without prompting, Petro suddenly put into words a thought I didn't even realize I'd been thinking. "Good years – I wonder if they aren't coming to an end?"

In surprise, I turned to look at her, and the expression on her face was just as shocked as mine was, the understanding of what she had voiced becoming suddenly clear to both of us.

"I didn't mean that!" she whispered in a flustered tone of voice.

"Hang on, though," I said. "Maybe you are absolutely right. Eight years is a long time to spend in the same place. Maybe we are at the end of a season here and it is time to move on. The church is well established, as is the Bible ministry. We have given what we came to give. Who's to say God isn't getting us ready for some kind of a move?"

"But I don't think I can leave Turkey right now." It was amazing to consider just how dramatically God had changed my wife's heart since those difficult early months in the country.

"Then let's not leave; Turkey is a big place, and there is still much work to be done in other parts of the country."

To my astonishment, the tranquil peace I had been enjoying earlier wasn't shattered by our ground-breaking discussion. Not only were my wife and I in complete – although unexpected – agreement, but it was as though the God whom we served was nodding and smiling right along with us, glad that we had received the message so quickly.

I reclined in my chair once again, determined not to miss the opportunity for a quick mid-afternoon snooze. "Time to move on, then," I murmured lazily. "I wonder where we will end up."

Just a few weeks later, we took to the road in our lovely minivan to attend a church camp at Lake Hazar in Central Turkey. This natural lake is the source of the Tigris River and offers a number of beautiful beaches for bathing, as well as attractive camping spots. Besides our own family, we were transporting quite a few of the other members from our church fellowship in Mersin. Even though we were a little squashed, we were enthusiastically enjoying the day trip.

Never having traveled through this particular region of Turkey before, I enjoyed observing the scenery, particularly the dramatic descent out of the arid mountains and into the fertile valley that was home to the city of Malatya. We cruised through quiet country roads lined by acreages of apricot trees, for which the district is famous, before entering the shady, well-tended boulevards of Malatya itself. Impressed by the tidiness of the streets and the abundant shrubbery, I thought it certainly could be very pleasant living in this city.

Almost immediately, I heard Petro exclaim from the back seat, "Wow – I could really live in a city like this!"

Startled, I turned to look at Petro, managing, much to the delight of the children in our group, to swerve the van a little in the process. She seemed oblivious to the fact that we had just been thinking exactly the same thing. Instead of sharing my joy at what appeared to be some direction from the Lord about our future, she nervously shouted and demanded that I quickly fix my eyes on the road again.

God spoke to me in dramatic ways at times in my life. Sometimes, though, He communicated by giving me gentle nudges in the right direction and a quiet sense of peace in my heart. This was one of those times. This coincidental thought, which both Petro and I felt in our hearts, together with our experience a few weeks before, now made me wonder whether God was not leading our family away from Mersin and on to Malatya.

Intrigued, I made a mental note to find out more about this captivating place.

Malatya, I later discovered, was another Turkish city steeped in history. A center of agriculture as far back as the Bronze Age, Malatya was an important city to both the Hittite and later the Roman empires. It was also a significant town for the traditionally Christian Armenian people and, until the early twentieth century, Armenians accounted for almost half of the population of Malatya. This changed in 1915, when, within just a few short months, up to 600,000 Armenian men, women and children across Turkey were killed in a state-sponsored genocide.

The Turkish government maintained that the deaths were a result of civil war and famine, but within Malatya itself, stories are still told of rivers running red with the blood of murdered Armenians and of seven young virgins who were impaled on wooden crosses in the main street. A once thriving Christian heritage came to an end in the 1960s, when the last remaining Christian Armenian moved to Istanbul.

Interestingly, Malatya is also the birthplace of Mehmet Ali Ağca, who attempted to assassinate Pope John Paul II in 1981.

As beautiful as the city was, with no missionaries and not a single believer even living there, Malatya was like an infertile spiritual desert, its soil eternally stained with the blood of Christian martyrs.

Lake Hazar, on the other hand, was now suddenly being inundated with believers. They benefited from the deep biblical teachings they shared and the Christian fellowship. Some had come from very far-flung regions of Turkey, just for the experience of being with other people of the same faith. Others, like a young Turkish man named Necati, came in search of God's direction in their lives.

Necati, his wife Semse and their two children were from the town of Izmir in the west of Turkey and worked with Campus Crusade for Christ in distributing Bibles. They were interested in expanding the reach of their ministry into the needy regions around the lake. The former accountant came from a Muslim background and turned to Christ after falling in love with Semse, an Orthodox Christian. The two of them married and went into ministry together. They faced extreme persecution in their hometown. Despite this, there was a real gentleness about them both and a certainty about God's calling in their lives.

One evening during the camp, I spent time observing the soft-spoken young Turkish man. A real diplomat, Necati had a way of calmly facilitating discussion between individuals, even when they were in disagreement, often helping them find common ground in their beliefs. During a particularly heated disagreement – when Turks disagree, it is definitely in a heated manner – between two Christians from different congregations, he graciously and in soothing tones led them back into understanding each other. I was impressed by his wisdom, and thought to myself that, should it be that God brought us to live and work in Malatya, Necati might be a very good co-worker.

Also at the camp, I once again bumped into quirky Tilmann. Maybe he had changed in the years since I had last seen him; maybe (and more likely) it was I who had changed. This time, instead of noticing only his idiosyncrasies, I saw more clearly his character strengths: a generous heart, dedication to the ministry, wisdom and a love for learning, as well as a true desire to see Turkey reached with the gospel. His wife Susanne shared his passion. She even had supposedly demanded, when Tilmann proposed marriage, that any husband of hers should not only be a dedicated Christian, but also one who wanted to live in a Muslim country. Petro and I spent much time in conversation with these two co-workers and once we had invested the time to really listen to their hearts and get to know them, we were much encouraged by the friendship we now shared.

Surrounded for days by such inspirational brothers and sisters, Petro and I found ourselves buoyed up in our faith. After much discussion and prayer, we seriously began considering moving to Malatya to begin a church planting ministry there. We shared the news with our friends in Mersin, as well as our support team in South Africa, and most of them responded enthusiastically. There was a definite consensus among all of us that this was what the Lord wanted. Heinrich, while sad to see us moving on after years of friendship, supported us in our decision.

There were, of course, the naysayers, as well as subtle hints every so often that not everything was going to be as easy as we might have hoped. In the local Hyundai dealership one day, while our treasured minivan was being serviced, the manager and I started talking about my work and our move to Malatya. At this stage, we had moved beyond the usual small talk, and he asked me exactly what kind of business I was involved in.

"Literature distribution," I answered truthfully.

Obviously this answer didn't provide enough detail for him, and he probed further. "What kind of literature?"

"Bibles, mostly," I responded with a smile. "Christian books and study guides."

He whistled, and raised his eyebrows in astonishment. "Christian literature, hey? I give you two years before you are well and truly famous in Malatya – or should I say *infamous*!"

He chuckled gleefully at his little joke, although I seriously doubted that in a city of nearly 800,000 people there was much chance of my becoming that well known. It just shows now how naïve I was at the time about what I could expect in that spiritually oppressed city.

Later that month, the family and I packed into the minivan on a scouting mission to Malatya. All of us, the boys included, were committed to the idea of pioneering new work in the region, and we had decided to investigate possible accommodation in the city as a team. It was exciting to include our children in the planning process for the first time and they, though sad about the idea of leaving friends and familiar surroundings behind, were keen to take a new step of faith for the Lord. Still not having learnt the lesson of traveling lightly, the minivan was crammed to the windows with all manner of things we might possibly need on a momentous occasion such as this.

We had trundled only 100 meters from our gate when disaster struck. I heard Benjamin cry out, followed by a sudden frenzy of frantic movement. I managed to pull over to the curb in time to see Petro trying to calm a hysterical Benjamin, whose whole foot had been doused in boiling-hot water from a supposedly spill-proof flask. Benjamin's screams filled the interior of the vehicle, and in an effort to help him, Petro recklessly pulled the sopping-wet sock from his foot. However, when she peeled off the sock, a whole layer of skin came away with it.

With screaming tires, the minivan skidded down the street to a clinic that was conveniently located within walking distance of our house. I jumped from my seat, rushed around to the side door of the vehicle and swung my son into my arms. Petro was hot on my heels as I ran in through the doorway of the clinic and begged the shocked nurses for attention. What had begun as a positive experience for us to share as a family was quickly turning into a serious nightmare.

Son medicated and foot delicately covered in gauze, we determinedly set out on our journey again a few hours later. Using the opportunity for a moment of spiritual instruction, Petro and I patiently explained to the three boys that it seemed perhaps not everyone was happy about our potential move to this Muslim stronghold, least of all the evil one. Our enemy wanted to thwart our plans to be obedient to God, even if that meant poor Benjamin ended up caught in the crossfire. We prayed together, committing our time in Malatya again to the Lord and asking for His protection.

With a rueful grin, Petro told Benjamin that he must feel pleased that God considered him ready to suffer for His name.

"I don't really care," my pragmatic son replied, his bandaged foot elevated on a stack of pillows on the seat beside him. "All I know is, it hurts."

Our earnest search for accommodation a few months later

culminated in the discovery of a massive home in one of the city suburbs. It was a three-story villa, with a large terrace and six huge bedrooms. Initially I emphatically turned down the estate agent's invitation to view it, as this looked nothing like any "missionary house" that I had ever encountered before. I wanted to suffer for the Lord, not live the high life! The agent was a convincing man, however, and persuaded us at least to have a look at it.

Keys in hand, we toured the spacious sitting-rooms and well-established gardens and realized that this would be the perfect setting in which to grow a new church. There was enough room to entertain visitors and we would always be able to extend hospitality to guests who might need a place to stay temporarily. While Petro was ecstatically admiring the gleaming kitchen appliances, I stepped out onto the patio to enquire of the Lord if this magnificent home was what He had in mind for us. It certainly wasn't what I had been expecting.

The Lord spoke to me, as I prayed on my own, and asked that I listen carefully. I already knew that the farmlands around Malatya were famous for their stone fruit, and that fresh as well as dried apricots were exported to areas throughout the world. In my mind's eye, I saw a picture of a pillar of apricots rising up high above the city, like a huge mushroom cloud. This unusual pillar and flying clouds of apricots first dispersed and then spread, like nuclear fallout, across Turkey, Europe and the entire globe. I sensed that the Lord was sending me a serious message in this vision, but didn't really understand it at the time. Only later did I come to realize that God was telling us that something, which would ultimately touch and affect the whole world, was going to happen in Malatya. Despite my doubts and the little acts of opposition we had faced, God reaffirmed our faith in His calling us to Malatya in this vision. It also gave us the confidence to go ahead and rent the beautiful house in which I was standing. I trusted that God knew we would need this home in order to minister effectively and accomplish the plans He had for us there.

Petro, by now happily admiring the spacious upstairs bathrooms, didn't need too much convincing.

As our plans to move out of Mersin really started to shift into high gear, we were faced with two dilemmas: who would replace us in Mersin when we left and who would go with us to support us in the new pioneering work in Malatya? God mercifully provided for us on both counts.

Stephan Smithdorf, a fellow South African, and his Japanese wife Keiko had served for some years on the OM ship *Doulos*. Nearly as old as the *Titanic*, and acknowledged in the *Guinness Book of World Records* to be the largest floating bookshop in the world, the *Doulos* sailed around the globe, its team doing evangelism, providing aid to poor nations and distributing quality literature. After a number of years living on the high seas, Stephan and Keiko were interested in becoming involved in ministry on land.

During an exposure visit to Turkey, Stephan and I were traveling between Izmir and Mersin by bus, with a bag full of audio cassettes containing Christian teaching material for the church. It was an overnight journey and the bus made a few stops during the night.

On our arrival at the side of the road in Mersin, I searched the luggage hold for my cassettes in vain. They had disappeared. I asked for help from the bus driver, who dispassionately brushed my protests aside and made his way back to the driver's seat. It was only when I raised my voice, demanding his attention, and started performing a loud dance of protest there by the side of the road, that he felt persuaded to help me out a little. He joined me in searching for the lost luggage, pulling bags out of the hold and putting them down on the dusty roadside for my inspection. Still there was no sign of the precious tapes. It seemed as though a dishonest fellow passenger had absconded with the bag during one of our stops. He most probably did not know what it contained. I told myself that quite likely the offender needed the Christian teaching much more than our little congregation did and so allowed the bus driver finally to return to his post and resume the journey.

Stephan, who had observed the dramatic scene, turned to me with a shocked expression on his face and said, "I had no idea you could get so angry!"

I just laughed, and explained that in Turkey, if you didn't learn to be vocal in the way you interacted with people, they would not take you seriously. Even Jesus, in a similar Middle Eastern culture, had sometimes voiced his dissatisfaction with people quite loudly. The secret was not to allow yourself to sin by acting wrongly in your anger.

Despite that rather harrowing experience for the normally reserved Stephan, he and his wife committed to the ministry in Mersin, and agreed to take on the responsibility of the Kayra office when Petro and I finally moved out. A local Turkish believer, Levent, committed himself to working with them and assisting in the business side of things. We were very pleased with the arrangement, especially because missions are widely regarded as institutions in which, if you want to move on, you need to find your own replacement!

Meanwhile, our new team in Malatya was slowly coming together, clearly under the direction of God. Necati, the young Turk I had met at church camp earlier in the year, contacted us, saying he had heard we were planning on moving further into the east of Turkey. He and his wife, though working with another mission agency at the time, were keen to come on board and join us when we started our work there. I was very pleased that we would be able to count on the pastoral gifting of this young man in our new field.

Then, one evening, I received a mysterious phone call from Tilmann. In hushed tones, he requested a personal meeting with me, explaining that he didn't want to discuss anything further with me over the telephone, in case his telephone had been bugged. A few days later, at a coffee shop in Mersin, he revealed that he and his wife, with their three children, wanted to join the team we were putting together. I was surprised, as I had never even told my plans to either him or his wife, let alone asked them to consider working with us. It was clear, however, that God was behind it all and I enthusiastically welcomed them aboard.

The two members who would complete our group felt compelled to join us in much the same surprising way. Angus Reed, a small, bald-headed Brit, and his wife Elizabeth worked with a mission organization called New Horizons. They were responsible for making contact with people in the east of Turkey who had shown interest in the Bible correspondence course. In this manner, they had come into contact with a young man named Hussein.

Hussein had been born physically disabled and because of this his movements were restricted to a stooped, scissor-like walk. In the Muslim culture, disability is viewed as a curse from God and he faced ridicule and ostracism from his community on a daily basis. Completely disillusioned by Islam for this reason, he began searching for the truth in other places. This search culminated in his requesting a New Testament from Angus through the mail system. Before Angus could take the relationship any further, this hurting Turkish boy, seemingly of his own initiative, knelt by his bedside alone and committed his life to Jesus. Thrilled, Angus and his wife continued their contact with him and began planning to move to the boy's hometown, so that they could continue in discipling him.

He lived in Malatya.

By chance, they heard that we were also in the process of moving to the region and they too requested to join our team, without any pressure on my part. It seemed that God was going ahead of us, preparing His own special dream team, without any assistance from Petro or me. There were now four families, from four different mission agencies and of four nationalities, whom God had called to begin something new in a significant region of Turkey. Our faith was strengthened by the knowledge that there was already a first convert, whom God had called to faith before we were even physically present in the city! It seemed as though we were all on the right path.

All the while, the authorities were well aware of our plans and movements. In order to keep my Turkish visa, I needed to register my business in Malatya so that we could live there legitimately. One morning, well dressed and hoping to make a good impression, I managed to find the right government building in which to lodge my application and respectfully approached the long reception counter, behind which a government official was lazily perusing the sports section of the newspaper.

For the briefest moment, he looked up to greet me, and then casually stated, "Oh, yes, you must be Martin de Lange, from Kayra."

I was astonished by this remark, as I had no idea how he could know my identity. I had never been to this office, nor met this man before. Tapping his forehead with two fingers in a gesture indicating that he knew all about me, he slid a pile of forms across the desk at me and said, "Fill these out for your tax registration," before returning his attention to the newspaper.

Not only was the government closely monitoring our movements, but the local media had also turned their attention to us when they got wind of the team of Christian missionaries descending on their Muslim community. They began reporting about Petro and me in the newspaper almost as soon as our family moved into our spacious new home in April 2003. Although the neighbors didn't seem very upset about suddenly having Christians on their street, the juicy little piece of gossip about our presence spread throughout the district quickly. Tilmann and Susanne managed to fare even better than Petro and I, featuring in a front-page report in the paper even before they had officially moved in.

"Congratulations!" I said to Tilmann over the phone, holding the article in my hand. "You made it onto the front page of the newspaper. Now everyone knows that the dangerous Christians are on their way to Malatya!"

Somehow, he didn't seem nearly as amused as I was.

Our presence well and truly confirmed in the city, the police began what proved to be a relentless mission to try to intimidate us, all the while keeping a very close eye on what we were doing. They rented the house across the street from us, and watched us during all hours of the day through gaps in their curtains. Close contacts of mine were dragged into police stations to be interrogated and bullied. When my home computer mysteriously became infected with a virus, I took it to a local technician to be fixed, only to discover later that the police had arrived at his shop minutes after I left with a warrant to seize all the documentation on the hard drive!

Through all this, the team sensed that on a spiritual level something very significant was happening in Malatya. We faced unending attempts by the enemy to frighten and discredit us, but also constant encouragement from God that He was with us and in control of the situation. If anything, the struggles we were facing from day one actually spurred us on and filled us with enthusiasm for the work of God in the city.

During our first year in Malatya, my main focus as team leader was not growing a strong church, although the church planting, evangelism and discipling ministries were always part of our daily work, but developing a sense of strong team dynamics between my co-workers.

Angus was the team administrator. He and his wife had MA degrees from Cambridge, and had an appreciation for structure and organization. It was refreshing to have someone finally to assist me in keeping everything together. A Bible translator and consultant, Angus was a logical thinker and did very well in developing protocols for our ministry, as well as trying to ensure we all followed them.

Necati, on the other hand, was more creatively and socially oriented, and sometimes struggled to follow these protocols. He was well known for not adhering to our established routine of testing seekers' motivations for investigating Christianity before allowing them to join our congregation. He often turned up at church on Sunday with two or three new friends without warning, informing us that he had a "good feeling" about them. He had a real heart for people and, perhaps in view of his background, great compassion for those lost in the lies of Islam. This difference in strategy might have been an obstacle between Necati and Angus, but they worked hard to keep communication lines open between them, and in many ways their natural abilities complemented each other.

It was quite easy for me to get to know these two better. My shy, introverted German co-worker required a little bit more effort on my part. He was a deep man and I longed to plumb those depths and get to know him more intimately. I finally found a solution when I discovered an interest we shared: cycling.

Twice a week, in the early morning when the first rays of the sun were still busy chasing away the shadows of the night, we would meet outside his home on our bicycles and begin a grueling cycle run of fifty kilometers on the idyllic country roads surrounding Malatya. With his penchant for precision, he rode a bike he had especially imported from his homeland.

He would take the lead straight away, cycling fast, even up the steep inclines of the rugged mountainsides, pushing himself always to greater levels of personal endurance. I would follow behind more sedately, comfortably riding in his slipstream, occasionally shouting in German, *"Du must langsamer fahren!"* – which I quite quickly learnt was a plea for him to ride a bit more slowly. Along the way, we would breathlessly talk about what was going on in our lives – issues at church, questions about faith, family situations – and I would experience a deep level of connection with him.

I grew to love this man, who had so utterly confused me in the beginning, as a brother. He was someone who never gave up; who fought battles with tireless endurance. I first discovered these character traits of his as I watched him pedal his bicycle along mountain paths, but gradually became aware of them in other areas of his life as well. I appreciated the dedicated, faithful role he played in our team in Malatya, and came to depend upon him greatly, as both a colleague and a friend.

We all understood the risks involved in missionary work in Turkey and took active steps to protect our families and ourselves. However, we also knew that God was sovereign and that He was ultimately responsible for our safety. During a weekend team retreat at Lake Hazar, early on in our time working together, I was able to share with them my personal struggle with fear. I told them how I constantly needed to guard against allowing it to become a hindrance to my effectiveness in preaching the gospel. Not surprisingly, I was not the only one in the team who admitted to having this problem. Amazingly, though, among the eight adults of our four families, six admitted that their greatest fear was to be caught in an earthquake! I was quite shocked to discover that, like me, most of the others were more concerned about being stuck underneath a collapsed home than being tortured for their faith.

Realizing the importance of handing this fear over to the Lord, we bowed our heads together in prayer. At that exact moment, the room around us began to shake. Our glasses of water spilled across the table and the all-too-familiar rumble of shaking foundations became unbearably loud. In panic, we each rose from our seats and dashed out of the room to look for our children and wait anxiously for the earth to stop shaking.

It had been a "small" quake for that region of Turkey, perhaps registering only about five on the Richter scale, but it had been enough to reveal just how deeply our fears ran and to help us to acknowledge our helplessness in keeping ourselves and our families entirely secure at all times. We finished our prayer outside, acknowledging the intensity of our need for God, but also our willingness to expose ourselves to dangerous situations for His sake.

Our team continued to bond deeply with one another and while some might have had doubts about our strategy and wondered why we didn't start concentrating on our evangelism ministry sooner, we truly believed that our work would bear more fruit if we were unified in what we were doing. We spent much time simply talking to one another, resolving issues and drawing up plans for the future. We wanted to have a solid foundation of four families aligned closely with one another before we considered adding more to our numbers. This later proved to be the best approach. After one year of establishing ourselves in the region, the ministry really took off and grew exponentially over the following two years. Whereas the church in Mersin had been rather sluggish in its growth at times, in Malatya our living-room was soon regularly packed with new believers. Dozens of people came to the Lord through correspondence courses and we were able to disciple a number of individuals and families personally.

One such family were Ali, Kudret and their three children. They lived in a tiny farm village named Dogan Shehir, a few kilometers outside Malatya. Like his father and grandfather before him, leathery-skinned Ali was a follower of folk Islam, grew apricots on a small farm and lived in a modest brick home of the customary design: a small, central living area, surrounded by four rooms housing a kitchen, a bathroom and two tiny bedrooms. They were neither rich nor poor, but very content with life.

Ali's sister had become a believer in the city of Ismir and I met her once when she was visiting Malatya. Desperate for her family to know the risen Savior, she took me to their home and introduced me to them. Over the following two years, we met with them weekly and shared studies from the Bible with them, highlighting key passages about Jesus and allowing them to ask questions. As the evenings grew cold, we would sit around the small coal brazier they kept in the center of the living-room, warming our hands and discussing the issues of life. Occasionally, I would take the rest of my family to their lovely rural village for the weekend, and as we grew closer to them, they included us in their lives more and more, even allowing us to help them with the annual apricot harvest. My boys ate as much of the fruit as they packed into the boxes, and I enjoyed working side by side with Ali.

Finally, one evening after another deep discussion, Ali clasped his heavily calloused hands together across his chest, nodded his head and cryptically said, "It is time."

"Time for what?" I asked.

"Time to give my life to Jesus."

As often as I had the privilege to experience moments like this, I never grew tired of them. A thrill coursed through my body and my heart pumped wildly in anticipation.

"Kudret!" I called out to Ali's wife, who was busy in the kitchen. She appeared at the doorway a moment later, her hands sticky with bread dough and her head covered modestly by a simple scarf.

"Your husband has decided that it is time for him to follow Jesus. What about you?"

With the familial submission expected of a Turkish housewife, but also with true love born out of many years toiling together side by side, Kudret came and knelt next to her husband. "If my husband is ready, then I too am ready," she said resolutely.

Ali grinned at his wife, took her hand and then bellowed for the three children to come and join them. They bounded into the room, not quite understanding what was going on, but caught up in the excitement of it all. Giggling every so often, they also knelt with their parents and prayed with me as together they all confessed their sins and gave their hearts to the Lord Jesus.

Echoing the words of Joshua, Ali looked at me, the lines in his face already seeming less severe and deeply furrowed, and said, "There now, it is done. My family and I will serve the Lord."

Chapter 8

Life was good.

After three years in Malatya, we had very little to complain about. Admittedly, the police harassment became a little tedious at times, but otherwise we were experiencing real success in the ministry. We were also quite comfortable living in the city. The boys were happily enrolled in good local schools, we had many friends, and relationships among the members of our team were good.

I had even managed to achieve something I had always struggled with: a good balance between work and home life. I had many meetings with new contacts, was distributing Bibles right across the region and helping to counsel new believers. However, I also spent enough time having fun with my wife and children – camping, cycling and enjoying their company.

The joy inherent in my life made the bleakness I saw in the residents of Malatya even more apparent. Walking to work one blustery winter's morning, I noted how the well-kept, landscaped gardens in the city parks contrasted starkly with the dull, grey clothing of the people on the streets. Eyes downcast, their faces and even the stoop of their shoulders hinted at the depressive malaise which hung over them like a heavy, wet blanket. There were still relatively few of them actively searching for the truth; but those who did seek God experienced real freedom and hope, and we saw them grow quickly and with enthusiasm in our little church.

With cold fingers, frozen in the blustery Anatolian winter, I unlocked the door of my office and the wind blew me inside. To my relief, I saw no sign of entrance by any unwelcome visitors such as local police officers. My paperwork didn't appear to have been disturbed during the night. Switching my computer on, I pottered around the room for a few minutes while it started up, putting the teapot on the gas stove in expectation of potential visitors dropping in, and tidying up a bit.

The literature distribution arm of our ministry had been doing exceptionally well recently, with many new bookstores coming on board and ordering stock. Eager to see whether our bank account was reflecting this growth – even in the world of missionary work money is essential to make things work – I sat down in my office chair and logged on to our internet bank account.

The balance of the account was zero.

Confused, I hit the "refresh" button, and even tried logging off and then on again. Nothing changed. Overnight, our very healthy bank balance had disappeared. Literally thousands of dollars had been sucked down a cyber drain.

Frantically, I clicked on the "transactions" button, hoping to find some clue about what had happened to our missing nest egg. I became even more confused when I saw, in our account history, a single lump payment from the Kayra account to that of Keiko Smithdorf, the wife of Stephan, who worked for Kayra in Mersin. Were I to imagine a person likely to turn rogue thief, this quiet, unassuming woman would always have featured last on my list of possibilities. Anxious to find some answers to the puzzle, I called Stephan, who was enjoying a short holiday with Keiko.

"Our money has gone *where*?" he gasped, once I had tried to explain the situation to him. Barely able to control my own rising panic, I reassured him that I was not trying to assign blame, only trying to discover what had happened.

"We haven't even had access to the internet the last few days," he muttered to himself, thinking aloud. "I had no idea… The site is secure. It must be an inside job, because they put the money into *Keiko's* account. But the only other person with access to our account and all our details is—"

"Levent," I interrupted grimly.

There was a groan from the other end of the phone. "I *knew* something was up. He hasn't been attending church regularly, and has been saying some odd things, becoming angry easily. But I wanted to give him the benefit of the doubt and left him in charge… with all our details within arm's reach."

"It's not your fault. He's made his own choices. I'm going to have to report him to the police."

Stephan, his holiday ruined, agreed to head back to Mersin to try to clean up the mess from there. I reluctantly headed down to the local police station. This time, I did not go as someone who had been arrested. I sadly went to report a crime suspected to have been committed by a friend, a brother in Christ, from our own congregation. For both Stephan and me, the loss we suffered through the betrayal of a friend far outweighed that of a few thousand dollars.

The plot thickened. Levent had completely disappeared, leaving behind only an administrative mess and the distinct impression that he had chosen to turn his back on the Lord. One of our company cell phones had gone missing with him, and we were continually charged for lengthy conversations to the phone numbers of clients. Finally, a police officer arrived at my office one morning and asked that I come down to the station to make a statement. Our company was being charged with harassment, due to some threatening phone calls that had been received by booksellers with whom we worked. Whatever his reasons were, Levent was angry enough to hurt not only us, but also the people who were our clients. Unusually sympathetic, the officers accepted my tale of woe, but insisted that until Levent reappeared, the charges against Kayra would stand.

Had this happened at any other time, I might have been able to brush it off as just a minor inconvenience. The betrayal of Levent hurt, certainly, as did the loss of all that money. We had lost face with many of our clients, and had to set to work restoring relationships and apologizing for the damage which had been done. Yet, in the grander scheme of things, these were small issues.

The big issue was that we were in the process of reapplying for our residency permits.

"Not completed," the burly visa official stated brusquely when I enquired about our applications. "Come back next week."

"I came last week already," I protested. "And the week before that. When will my permit be granted?"

"It says here in your file that there are open charges against you. Your visa application has been put on hold, pending further investigations."

"What investigations?" I cried. "I've explained everything to the police. I am not the one who has committed a crime; I am the victim! You can't use this as an excuse to deny me the right of living in this country."

His huge hands sliding my receipt back across the desk towards me, he muttered through his teeth, "Come back next week," and turned to the next person in the queue.

Crushed, I realized that this was not a battle I could fight on my own. No matter how hard I struggled on my part, there was no way in which I could force the hands of government officials obviously determined to use this unfortunate situation as a means to kick me out of the country. I knew in my heart that this was an issue to be resolved by God and God alone. Surely He knew that we needed to be in Malatya, saw the good work that we were doing here and would make a way for us in His own, perfect time. I made a conscious decision to wait on Him to move on our behalf.

I waited for a really, really long time.

Week after week, I returned to the police station to collect our permits. Week after week, I returned home to Petro without them. At first, I was hesitantly optimistic, but as the weeks continued to roll by, I became emotionally crushed. By now, our permits to live in the country had actually expired, but we chose to keep waiting anyway. Petro and I prayed together, fasting and appealing to God to help us. Despite the challenging situation, we trusted that God would answer our prayers.

After four agonizing months, He did answer, but it wasn't the answer for which we had been waiting. The head of the provincial police department informed us abruptly that we were now considered illegal residents in Turkey.

We broke the news to the boys over dinner one evening. Martin, shell-shocked, sat quietly in his chair, waiting for some kind of explanation. Benjamin stabbed testily at the carrots left on his plate, while Samuel, overcome, bleated, "They can't make us leave – can they?"

"They can," I shrugged. "They've decided we can't stay, and there's no fighting it. We have to go."

"Go where?" Martin asked.

Petro and I glanced at one another, unsure of how to answer. "We don't know yet," I replied. "God must want to use us in a new place—"

"Why can't God just let us stay *here*?" Samuel cried.

"I don't know, son. I don't understand either. However, we will just have to trust that He knows best and listen to His guidance. Maybe He wants to send us to a new country. Maybe it is time for us to go home to South Africa…"

Benjamin stopped butchering his vegetables long enough to cast a fierce look across the table at me. "South Africa doesn't feel like home. I wasn't even born there—"

"Or me!" Samuel interjected.

"—I've only really visited on holidays. I don't have any friends there. Turkey is home." He paused, overcome for the moment. "I am Turkish."

The brutal truth about the realities faced by missionary children dawned on me right then. This wasn't a life my children had chosen. They had been willing participants in the process, but it had been the burden on their parents' hearts which had taken them on this journey. Our children had spent all their lives on the mission field, making sacrifices of which they often weren't even aware and living a complicated life that had been thrust upon them and for which they had not asked.

Yet my children also possessed a deep resilience and had a relationship with God completely unlike that of their peers in South Africa. They had seen God put to the test and proven almighty. Maybe life hadn't always been comfortable for them, but they had developed strength of character, which I knew would serve them well in their walk with the Lord. My three young boys had proven themselves warriors in God's hands and I allowed myself to accept that, even if this process was going to be painful for them, God knew what was best for them.

"You are allowed to be disappointed," I told my three kids. "I am disappointed too. However, I know that God will not leave us to work all this out on our own. He is with us, and He has great plans for us."

The sentiment expressed was pleasant enough, but it was a truth even I had difficulty accepting. So much of my identity, for the majority of my adult life, had been established in my life and ministry in Turkey. The very idea of moving forward to something new terrified me and broke my heart at the same time. I would wake up in the middle of the night, drenched in sweat and weeping, with a concerned Petro at my shoulder trying to calm me. I felt as if I were falling off a cliff, with no idea if there would be something to break my fall before I hit the bottom.

I knew I needed to hear from God. Surely He was speaking to me and wanting to guide me, but perhaps I was not listening carefully enough. I did what I always do when I want to seek God's face: I decided to get my body moving. I took a bus down to Mersin, from where I set out on a three-day bicycle tour along the Turkish coastline with the intention of devoting my time to finding out what God had in store for my family and me.

It was a life-changing experience. My body complained in exhaustion as I pushed myself to greater levels of physical endurance than I had ever before experienced. Up and down dusty paths, through craggy mountains I rode, causing tendons, joints and muscles to rebel in pain. At times, thick sheets of rain pummeled my body, and all of my gear was drenched in water. Then the hot desert winds would move in, sucking up each last drop of moisture and leaving me parched. Somehow, it felt as though the Lord needed me to be removed from all of the other voices competing for attention in my life. Then He would step in and whisper to me the guidance and assurance I so desperately needed. It was God and I, head to head, alone together in the wilderness.

On the third night, as I camped on the rocky roadside in the drizzling rain, I noted everything I was experiencing in my journal. The soft glow of my torch provided just enough light in my small tent to make writing possible. I filled page upon page with questions to God.

It was definitely not a matter of not having any options of where to go and what to do. Petro and I had been inundated with offers from different churches and organizations to join them in their work. I was particularly partial to the idea of moving to Australia to assist a church there with ministry to Turkish immigrants. Another offer, to join the staff of a university in the UK and teach missiology – with a regular income to boot – also appealed to me. Yet I didn't experience any real peace about accepting either of these offers.

More than anything, I simply felt disappointed in God. It seemed as though everything was ending so badly and in such an uncomfortable way. Surely, after years of faithful service, we deserved some kind of credit and kindness for all we had done for Him.

That night, unable to sleep, in damp cycling clothes and aching all over, I finally received from the Lord the quiet, unwavering peace for which I had so desperately yearned.

"I know it hurts," He said, "but I am more concerned with your growth as a person than with your comfort. Let go, trust Me and go home to South Africa," He whispered into my heart, His voice a soothing balm in a time of true uncertainty. "It is time to go home."

With this reassurance, Petro, our three boys and I began the painful process of bringing closure to thirteen years in Turkey.

In April 2006, we started with the huge upheaval of moving back to a life in Africa. Eager to share this news with churches supporting our work in Turkey, I wrote letters explaining what we believed God wanted us to do, and asking for input and prayers. All of those on our support team unanimously indicated that we had correctly heard the voice of the Lord and whole-heartedly encouraged us to move ahead in our plans to come back home.

Thankful for their whole-hearted support, Petro and I spent long evenings bent over paperwork, trying to calculate exactly what it would cost to move our family of five across the world. Airfares were certainly not cheap; nor were the costs of shipping furniture and household goods by sea, securing a vehicle and housing once back in South Africa and getting three boys set up for school. Our budget was definitely not extravagant, but it was with quite a large degree of shock that Petro and I made the final calculations and realized that this venture would set us back more than 200,000 rands – about 30,000 US dollars.

Again, I contacted the churches which had sent and supported us, and informed them of our needs. All of a sudden, there was little sign of support. The general question, it seemed, was whether we didn't have a plan B.

There was no way that we would be able to come up with the cash to do this on our own. With just a hint of desperation, I reminded our support team that they would need to put their money where their mouths were, and come on board to help us relocate. Slowly and reluctantly, they came around, and money started to trickle into our relocation fund. After a few weeks we had managed to raise just 10,000 rands (1,500 US dollars), which was not even enough to pay for our flight tickets home.

Late one evening, I lay awake in bed, listening to the soft sounds of Petro asleep next to me. Again, I was finding it difficult to trust God. He had taken us on some wild journeys and had always provided for our needs, but I had no idea how He intended to pull this off. We needed to leave the country, for legal reasons, as soon as possible. Yet God seemed to be dragging His feet in making this possible.

"I want to trust You, Lord," I prayed quietly. "But You aren't exactly proving Yourself very trustworthy at the moment. We need so much money, but You have only given us a little. What am I supposed to do with just 10,000 rands?"

The instructions I received from the Holy Spirit at that moment were enough to set my stomach lurching: "Give it away."

I believe in generosity, don't get me wrong. My family had been at the receiving end of people's cheerful giving for many years, and we in turn had tried to incorporate generosity as an important part of our lifestyle as well. However, for people who so desperately needed this money, at so desperate a time, the idea seemed laughable. Only five minutes earlier, 10,000 rands had seemed like such a pitiable sum of cash; now, as God challenged me to sow the largest sum I had ever given away in my life, I only saw a big zero written in a vibrant red marker on the whiteboard of my mind.

I woke Petro, maybe looking for some kind of absolution from guilt rather than advice. "Speak to me through my wife," I begged God, as Petro sat up, sleepily rubbing her eyes. "Use her to show me that this bizarre idea comes from the enemy, and not from You."

"We have to go for it, though, don't we?" she stated matter-of-factly, when I had explained the situation to her, even emphasizing the sheer ridiculousness of the idea. "I mean, you can't just ignore God and hope He'll still provide for us. Give it away."

Calmly, she rolled back onto her side and fell straight back to sleep, leaving me to worry and fidget for the rest of the night over the size of the task God had given me.

In the morning, I faced the situation and rang a colleague who was working with OM in Istanbul. Reluctantly, I explained our situation, and told him that some time in the early hours of the morning I had been given the distinct impression that I needed to send the whole 10,000 rands to him.

I heard sobbing from the other end of the phone line. Between gulps, he explained to me that he was also moving, and needed exactly that sum of money to move his family to a new region in Turkey. He had been begging the Lord to provide and now, it seemed, God had done just that.

It was an answer to prayer for him, but with my bank account once again at zero, this was just a confusing puzzle to me.

Surely I should have known by then that God does not abandon His children. We didn't receive the lump sum we needed to pay for all our expenses at once. I definitely would have preferred it this way. It certainly would have been easier to trust God with the assurance of a comfortable, big figure of 200,000 rands in my bank account. Instead, little by little, as each new bill for our international move was delivered to our mailbox, we would also discover just enough money to remain free of debt. Our airfares were paid, just in time. We hired a moving company in Malatya to help Petro pack all our furniture and other household goods in boxes, and I just had enough funds to hand over their fee on their last day of work. The quote I was given to ship our container by sea showed amazing correlation to the small amount of credit I discovered in our bank account one day. Day by day, God gave us our bread, as well as what we needed in order to be obedient to Him.

Martin Junior, who had almost overnight grown into a striking, robust teenager, accompanied me on a trip to Istanbul to see our container of furniture through customs. We had to complete never-ending piles of paperwork to be stamped and signed before permission would be granted for the container to be loaded onto a ship and sent back to South Africa. We spent a successful morning together, trudging from office to office, acquiring the necessary permissions and making sure little squiggles of blue ink adorned each dotted line on our papers.

We made it to the harbor in the late afternoon, pleased to see our bright-red steel box on the docks. It held all our earthly belongings, and it had been quite a feat to pack it. We had hired experts to assist us in this and it was done so well that we would not have been able to fit in another item.

I was feeling confident at this stage, pleased that we had managed to finish our day's work with only one more signature from the harbor-master required. Smugly, I handed my documents over to the official in the front office, asking for his help in finishing our paperwork.

"I'm afraid I can't do that," he said, pointing to the visa stamp in my passport. "Your residency permit expired more than six months ago. You are not legally entitled to export goods from Turkey."

Martin Junior gave a low whistle and shook his head. "Mom's not going to be happy…"

I did my best to negotiate. I cajoled, begged and threatened, but it seemed as though there was no budging the man, or skirting the regulations. The very most he could offer me was to open up the container and check what was inside, but this would have necessitated hiring a crew to do the unpacking and repacking, a luxury we could not afford. Quietly, I asked Martin to pray.

Suddenly, the official decided it was necessary to take my passport up to the commissioner for inspection. He strode off through the big, dank building and I hurried along after him, hoping not to be separated from this important piece of documentation. Briskly, he stepped into a big office, with me trailing closely behind, and stood to attention before an important-looking official. An official who looked both important and strangely familiar.

Suddenly, I recalled his name. It was Naji. While I struggled to determine how exactly I knew him, I momentarily saw the same expression of slight confusion on his face, before his eyes lit up in joyful recognition.

"Martin!" he cried out. "Can it really be you? Neighbor! How long has it been? Ten years?"

He leapt up from his seat and embraced me in his strong arms, as I laughed and kissed his face. Hundreds of kilometers away from where we had first met, I had managed to bump into the man who had lived next to my family during our first years in Mersin. Our children had played on the lawn together and our wives had exchanged stories on the sidewalk. While it had been a long time since we had parted ways, the bond of friendship we had shared was as strong as ever.

"You look good, Naji!" I grinned. "It seems this job is good for your health."

"That would be my wife's cooking, actually! However, the job is great. We earn a lot more here than we ever could have in Mersin, and it is nice to be in charge…"

He looked briefly at the puzzled young official, who still stood to attention with my passport in his hand.

"What's the problem here?" he asked, authority evident

in his voice. He snatched up the passport, flicked through it briefly and then indicated that he wanted to see my papers. I handed them to him quickly, enjoying watching him make a show of the influence he commanded in this office. With a flourish, he stamped my papers, signed them and thrust them back at the now completely stunned officer.

"Done," he smiled at me. "Have a safe journey. It has been wonderful to see you again."

I agreed, reflecting on just how incredible my God is, that He would give this one man a promotion in order for him to ensure that my household furniture could return to South Africa with me.

While it was exciting to witness God performing amazing miracles to help us on our journey, perhaps some of the more memorable moments that strengthened our faith were seemingly trivial issues which needed to be sorted out in our relocation. One of these situations came in the form of our pet dog, Snoopy.

Snoopy was a real character. She possessed all the charm and rambunctious energy of a street urchin, because deep down that was what she really was. In our early years in Mersin, the boys had begged us for a pet, and as I had fond memories of frolicking through my childhood accompanied by a cheerful mutt or two, I agreed. I had my heart set on a lovely pure-bred dog, perhaps a retriever of some kind, or an obedient sheepdog, but these breeds were very expensive in Turkey. In Muslim culture, dogs are considered unclean, unholy animals. In fact, if you really want to insult someone, you will call him or her a dog. For this reason, pet dogs are not readily available.

This is not to say that dogs are not common in Turkey. There are many dogs, but most live on the streets. Born wild, scrawny puppies grow into vicious pack animals, roaming the neighborhoods looking for food and terrorizing the children. Often, with the local government doing nothing to control the situation, community members take matters into their own hands and round up the feral dogs to be killed.

On one of our daily trips to the local kindergarten, Martin Junior and Benjamin stumbled on a litter of six-week-old puppies. Bitten by fleas and undernourished, they were definitely not beautiful, but the boys begged me to keep one, and I relented. Symbolically, we picked out the smallest dog, a pitiful little runt, to keep as a reminder of how God chooses the weak and makes them strong.

Our little "pavement special", or Snoopy as she came to be known, quickly became a member of our family. Her frame filled out healthily and her ragged black-and-white coat thickened, although she never completely lost the ruffian look with which she had been born. She loved nothing more than a good gambol with our children in the back yard and her wagging tail would set her whole body into motion when she was pleased to see someone.

When our return to South Africa became imminent, I searched desperately for a new home for Snoopy. Of course, none of our Muslim neighbors felt the same kind of affection for a pet dog as we did. Even the believers in our church were less than enthusiastic. Shipping Snoopy back to South Africa was too expensive an option for us to consider and so I regretfully took Snoopy to the vet to see what he might suggest. While I had thought putting Snoopy gently to sleep was the most humane of solutions, the vet scoffed at it, said I was being cruel, and that I should rather turn her out onto the streets. I knew, though, that there was no way our spoilt princess would survive back in the "wild".

With three weeks until departure, the boys were getting

desperate and I still had no plan as to how to redeem the situation. Finally, at the last minute, my parents called from South Africa to say they would somehow find a way to pay the exorbitant fee to have Snoopy flown to our new home with us. In a frantic rush to get everything completed in time, I hired an agent to help me with the paperwork for the dog, and bought a crate and the necessary medication to ensure that Snoopy's trip, if not a first-class journey, would at least be bearable.

She arrived the day after us, and eager to bring her home I set out early on a Saturday morning to a big cargo warehouse in Johannesburg. A less than enthusiastic state vet greeted me, informed me that my paperwork was all wrong and said he had no choice but to send Snoopy back to Turkey. Try as I might, I could not convince him that, although we had been in the country for thirteen years, there was nobody in Turkey who would accept the dog. Faced with the realization that we could not possibly afford to ship her by plane again, I begged him to consider putting her down. However, it seemed I had again encountered an animal doctor who thought the option cruel. Once again, I was stuck in an impasse.

Relenting slightly, he agreed to let me out into the storage shed to visit poor Snoopy. Shivering with shock, she sat chained to her crate, head bowed in defeat, looking up at me with big and pleading eyes. It was more than I could bear to see her in such a pitiful state. I fondled her head and ears sadly, and huge tufts of fur fell out because of the stress she was enduring.

I decided to take matters into my own hands. Seeing a choker chain hanging on the wall of her cage and feeling I had no other option for relieving her from this misery, I slipped it gently over her head, with the intention of tightening it until she passed out and slipped away. Whispering soothing words to her, I was about to pull tightly onto the chain to choke her, when I heard God speak to me.

"Stop!" He said. "Where there is life, there is hope."

Never before had God spoken to me so clearly, and I quickly put the chain away, patted Snoopy on the head once again and walked out of the building. I would just have to allow God to fight on our behalf.

Later that afternoon, the same uncooperative vet called to say that he had changed his mind, and if our dog passed her quarantine tests, he would release her to us the coming Friday. I had very nearly killed our dog in a misguided attempt to fix my own problems, yet God had proven again that He was very much in control. Our boys, although less than impressed when they heard what I had almost done, were thrilled that God had made a way for them to get their dog back. Snoopy joined our family once again a few days later, and with mad cavorting and joyful leaps demonstrated that all had been forgiven.

However, that was all yet to come. Back in Turkey, we were faced with the sad reality of bidding friends – many of whom had become like family – a final farewell. During our last church service, Petro and I looked at the many individuals who were now an important part of our lives. Their stories had become eternally threaded together with ours, and parting from them was mind-numbingly painful.

In a beautiful gesture, Hussein, our first disciple in Malatya, awkwardly carried a bucket of water to where Petro was seated and delicately removed her sandals. In tears, he gently washed her feet as a symbol of service, in the way that Jesus had done. Petro bowed her head to weep quietly, and we who were watching also cried. We were reminded of the many times that Petro had lovingly washed and tended to Hussein's disabled, callused and bruised feet as an expression of her care and compassion toward him.

I spent my last evening in Turkey down by the Euphrates River with my three team-mates. Angus, Necati, Tilmann and I resolutely tended the barbecue, enjoying the fragrant aroma of the lamb chops which hissed over the hot coals.

Tilmann, his face lit by the glowing flames, patted me on the shoulder as the four of us paused for a moment to pray together. Never before had I experienced such deep friendship and fellowship as I had with these three men. They had supported me through difficult times, shared in our moments of joy and challenged me in my walk with God. I had begun in ministry as their team leader; now it rather felt as if I were their brother.

At that moment, the sun was setting in brilliant orange hues on the horizon, much as it was setting on our time in Turkey. It symbolized the end of an era and we knew things would never be the same for us again. However, we trusted not only that God had more good things in store for us, but also that the many deep relationships we had built here in Turkey would only grow in years to come.

I raised my can of soda with a smile, bowed deeply to each of my three friends, and toasted them.

"My brothers forever!" I said.

Chapter 9

After six months back in South Africa, it seemed that we were finally getting used to the new realities of life. Re-entry, and the tumult of emotions that came with it, had been a shock to all of our systems. South Africa was not Turkey, nor would it ever be. The South Africa to which we returned in 2006 was also not the same as the country Petro, Martin and I had left in 1993. People and places previously familiar to us had changed in our absence and the very way of life had been transformed dramatically since we had last lived here. Although much had changed for the better, it took some time really to feel at home in what sometimes seemed like yet another foreign country.

Nevertheless, we eventually adapted to our new life. Within months, we had a new home, new friends, and new schools for the boys. In short, we had started a new life as a family. The role I was assigned in OM South Africa was to mobilize the church to become actively involved in missionary work. This I did by sharing my own personal experiences in the field. It was exciting and bearing much fruit. Ironically, after years of fearing for our personal safety in Turkey, Petro enjoyed the relative security we experienced in what is usually described as a "dangerous" country. The boys were even beginning to conduct their arguments in our new home not in Turkish, but in Afrikaans.

It is amazing, however, how your life can change completely, without any inkling of a warning, in an instant.

The 18th of April 2007 began just as any other day in our household. Petro sent the three sleepy boys off to school, while the sun was still making its slow ascent into the Pretoria skyline to warm the morning. I enjoyed my quiet time alone with the Lord for a little while longer after they had left. If He had been trying to warn me of what was happening thousands of kilometers away at that very moment, I did not notice it.

After a morning at the OM offices, scheduling church meetings for the weekend, I headed to collect Benjamin and Samuel from their school. I parked in the leafy street bordering the school and sat on the hood of the car to wait for them. Eventually, I caught sight of Samuel chatting to a group of friends at the front gate, with Benjamin behind him trying to hurry him along. I waved to them, indicating that they should hurry, as we still had to collect Martin Junior from his school.

My phone rang.

After a slight delay, a familiar voice came through the speaker. "Hi, Martin, this is Stephan."

"Stephan, my friend!" I exclaimed happily. "How are things in Mersin?"

Their bags slung casually over their shoulders, the boys finally made it to the car, and started squabbling over who could take the front seat.

"Martin, I'm sorry, but I have some bad news." Stephan's voice sounded tense, strained, as though he were trying to maintain his composure.

"They're dead, Martin. Necati and Uğur. And Tilmann.

Murdered in the office this morning. I am so sorry…"

For a moment, all I was aware of was my own beating heart, its rhythm suddenly becoming painfully frenzied within my chest. Dead? But I had seen them, all three of them, just a few short months ago. Necati and Tilmann, my co-workers, and Uğur, Necati's friend and the new member of the team.

I could still vaguely hear Stephan's voice speaking to me as if through a block of concrete.

"We still don't really know all the details. It happened this morning. I wanted you to hear it from us before it reaches the media. Martin, are you still there?"

"I'm here," I said, weakly. "Look, Stephan… I have to go. I'll call you later."

I climbed into the car, my legs weak and hands trembling. The boys stopped their arguing long enough to realize that something was wrong.

"Dad? Are you okay?" Benjamin asked.

"No. But I can't tell you now. Let's just go and collect your brother."

Somehow, functioning on autopilot, I managed to drive the car safely through the hectic traffic. I slowly worked my way towards Martin's school, aware of little else other than my own overwhelming grief.

This was the headline: "Murder in Anatolia – Christian Missionaries and Turkish Ultranationalism". This report by the European Stability Initiative on the murder of Christian missionaries in Anatolia and an investigation into Turkish ultranationalism, published in Berlin on 12 January 2011, as well as records of the court proceedings of the trial of the suspects later apprehended for this gruesome act, shed light on the events which led to the murders. The following scenes are what I imagine to have taken place in Malatya prior to the murders:

Earlier that morning five disillusioned young men met at a coffee shop in Malatya to finalize the terrible plans they had been working on for months.

"We do it today," Emre said, his breakfast plate growing cold in front of him as he excitedly confirmed the details of the plot to his friends. "I have the gloves, ropes and guns in the car. We are ready."

Cuma shook his head anxiously. "I don't see why we need the guns. Or the knives." He looked pointedly at Abuzer, who, he knew, was concealing the weapons in the large pockets of his jacket. "If the idea is just to get information, then why do we need to be so brutal?"

"That's never been the idea!" Emre hissed. "These people want to destroy our country and kill our children! Someone must stop them. Don't be a fool, Cuma. If we don't make the first move, then we are putting our own lives and families at risk."

Abuzer, Salih and Hamit all nodded in agreement.

"I swear to you, Cuma – you cop out now and I promise that if the Christians don't come after you, I will!"

Shocked by the vehemence of Emre's threat, the other four youths sat quietly for a few moments. Certainly, they knew of Emre's vicious tendencies – as boarders in the same university hostel, they had heard not only of how he had threatened and attacked other people in the past, but also how, through his links with high-profile members of the police force, he had managed to avoid arrest for crimes he had committed. In fact, both Hamit and Cuma had witnessed Emre stabbing other students on two separate occasions earlier that year. He then calmly cleaned himself before waltzing down to the local police station to ensure that no charges would be laid. Even now, the chilly cruelty in his tone was disturbing.

"You're sure they don't suspect anything?" Hamit eventually asked.

"Nothing," Emre grinned. "I've told you, I've got Necati completely fooled. He really thinks I am serious about converting. He even invited me to their church celebration the other day." He laughed. "Imagine – all of them sitting there, thinking I am one of them, while all the time I am imagining how easy it is going to be to slit their throats!"

He rose from his chair, motioning for Abuzer to follow. "Come on. Let's go check if it isn't time already. We will meet at the sports center. Until then, remember that Allah is happy with our plans – and so are my friends in the government!"

Petro was busy in the kitchen when I finally made it back to the house. The three boys, their faces ashen with worry, followed me in. I had heard their concerned whispering during the long drive home, and had known that my silence was very upsetting to them. However, I hadn't been able to face the idea of unleashing the torrent of emotions inside me until I was in a safe place – and inside my wife's arms was the safest place I could think of being at that moment.

Disturbed by the quietness of what was usually a boisterous entrance by my boys and me, Petro immediately knew that something was wrong. She was at my side in an instant, her hands to my face.

"Something terrible has happened…" I began. Then I couldn't hold out any longer.

"Oh God, help me! They are dead, Petro. Tilmann and Necati and Uğur. Stephan told me. They have been murdered. I don't know more than that, but it really happened. It's not a joke, and I can't bear it!"

"No…" Petro moaned. "Susanne and Semsa? Are they okay?"

I reached out to comfort her, but I myself was already a sobbing mess and could barely keep standing upright. The boys, probably no less shocked by seeing their parents in distress than by hearing such terrible news about our friends, began to cry quietly in the corner of the kitchen.

Managing to regain some composure, I phoned my parents and the director of OM in South Africa, asking them to come and support us immediately. Within minutes, they were on their way to our home, to be with us, comfort us and assist us in navigating through the next few difficult hours. Later, I was able to phone Stephan again. However, the details were sketchy still and nobody was quite sure what was going on, except that our three friends were dead. Understandably, the Christian community in Turkey was shocked by what had happened, and very, very afraid. I knew immediately that I needed to be there with them at this time. I was unsure of how it would even be possible, but I trusted God to make a way for us to return, if even briefly, to Turkey.

Hunched over five sheets of lined lecture paper, Emre, Hamit, Salih, Cuma and Abuzer sat together to write their last messages to their families.

"We are brothers. We go to our death," they wrote.

"We might not return. If we die, we will become martyrs; those that stay alive should help each other. Give us your blessings. We five are brothers, we are going to death, we might not return."

They prayed together briefly. Then, taking up their weapons, they tucked the letters into their pockets and began the short stroll down the street to the Kayra offices.

Petro and I couldn't sleep that night. Our feelings fluctuated between raw grief and concern about everything that needed to be worked out for our intended return to Turkey for the funerals. We spent much time in prayer, crying out to God for His help to make it possible for us to come to terms with what had happened that day.

Our question was not so much about why this had happened. Having lived in Turkey for thirteen years, we understood the risks and knew that all three of the men would have willingly laid down their lives for the sake of the gospel. Instead, we wondered why we were not among them. Why had we been spared and these three friends of ours slain? Why had God called us to leave Turkey, just a few short months before what would become the moment of greatest need for the church in Malatya?

That night, I wrote in my journal: "Yesterday was surely the most terrible day of my life. My three friends, Necati, Uğur and Tilmann, were murdered in my old office. They were killed for Jesus and His kingdom… They paid the ultimate price. The world was not worthy of them! I am proud to have been their brother and their friend."

Gokhan and his wife Gulshen, Turkish Christians who had been sent by the church in Ankara to strengthen the team in Malatya, immediately knew something was wrong. They had been standing at the locked office door for a long time, knocking, calling out and even phoning the office line, but with no answer. It seemed that none of the three men whom they had expected to meet today were available.

However, from inside the offices they could hear sounds of moaning.

Suspicious, they called the police, who to their amazement arrived within only a few short minutes. The next few moments were like scenes from a movie. The police banged on the door a few times, then decided to take drastic action and broke it down. There on the floor, Gokhan saw his three co-workers in a pool of blood, covered in stab wounds, their hands and feet bound and their throats slit.

The three murdered men were not alone in the office. Hamit, Salih and Cuma were apprehended then and there, their hands covered in the blood of the victims. Abuzer was discovered one floor below, on a balcony, trying to make a getaway. Emre, the mastermind behind the plot, was found injured on the pavement in front of the building moments later. He had fallen from the third floor in an attempt to escape.

It was a scene that Gokhan would never forget.

Petro and I saw God work in miraculous ways amid the bewilderment and haste of the following days.

Our plan was to fly back to Turkey to attend Necati's funeral, as well as to support our friends in the church in Malatya. Unfortunately, we would miss the funerals of Tilmann and Uğur. Obviously, though, this meant that we would have to get visas to enter Turkey. We also had to get a new emergency passport for Petro, whose old one had recently expired. Somehow, we had to raise the all-important cash for plane tickets as well. We had learnt to trust God for larger sums of money in the past, however, so it did not really surprise us when the money – more than 40,000 rands (5,500 US dollars) – needed for Petro and myself to fly to Malatya was raised in just a few short hours.

At the Turkish embassy in central Pretoria, we were met with nothing but sympathy from the staff. Despite the fact that the Turkish government had blacklisted me, Petro and I were granted temporary visitor visas to Turkey almost immediately. Perhaps more amazingly, Petro was granted her passport by the South African Department of Home Affairs in only one day!

News of what had happened in Malatya spread quickly, and within a day the internet was flooded with accounts of what had happened to my three friends, many of them untrue. Sadly, it seemed that even the international church had fallen prey to much of the hysteria generated by the media on the web and delighted in passing around gory and sensational stories of how the men had been tortured. For my part, I participated in a few radio and newspaper interviews in South Africa, focusing on the extreme heroism and love of my friends and the sacrificial way they had lived for Jesus, rather than the tragic manner in which they had died.

Meanwhile, news of our intent to visit Turkey had spread as far as the South African embassy in Ankara. Soberly, they phoned me on two separate occasions and requested that I not make the trip. "Your name is in all the newspapers," they explained. "We know it is important for you to be here, but we fear for your safety. Please do not come." I understood and appreciated their concern, but Petro and I would not waver in our desire to be in Turkey during that critical time.

After nearly two days of trying, I finally managed to get hold of Susanne on the phone. The new widow, still coming to terms with what had happened, was nevertheless incredibly calm and composed as she received our condolences and answered our questions about what had happened. She told us that Angus, whom we had not heard from in the preceding days, had disappeared with his family, after their details had been published in a local newspaper. I was sad that he had not remained behind to offer strength to the church and lead the remaining members of our team, but understood the enormous stress he must have been experiencing.

Susanne was too busy dealing with her own grief over what had happened to be overly upset by the departure of her friends. Irritated with Tilmann over something that had happened earlier that morning, Susanne had eventually tried to telephone him around lunchtime on the day he was murdered, but had not been able to get through. She had no idea that something was wrong, until a friend called later in the day to ask if she knew what had happened. It transpired that the police had notified the media of the attacks before even informing Susanne. She waited for hours at the local police station, begging for some kind of information, before they finally officially told her that her husband was dead.

Nobody would agree to bury Tilmann. Susanne wanted Malatya, the town where he had died, to be his final resting place, but now the local authorities were spreading rumors that it was a sin for a Muslim to dig a Christian's grave. Susanne, however, was resolute; Tilmann would be buried in Turkey.

Finally, volunteers from a church in another city agreed to dig a grave for him in a hundred-year-old, abandoned, Armenian cemetery.

Then the local media wanted a quote from the widow. She did not want to talk to them. Her grief was too new, too painfully raw to share with the rest of the world, but God strengthened her and inspired her with the words that His own Son had uttered from the cross: "Forgive them, because they don't know what they are doing."

In just one sentence, the media later reported, a brave woman did more for Christianity in Turkey than a thousand missionaries could have done in a thousand years.

On board an Olympic Airlines flight, via Athens to Istanbul, I was a mess of emotions. Petro and I were traveling alone, as our parents were taking care of the boys. We were relieved knowing that they were in capable hands. However, three days into the ordeal, I was still trying to deal with the waves of anguish that sometimes hit me unexpectedly throughout the day. Every so often, I would collapse into a fresh well of sorrow, mourning for my friends and feeling so guilty that I had not been there with them. It was probably a good thing that Petro and I had two seats next to the window to ourselves.

On the other hand, we were also excited to be returning to Turkey so quickly, to see some of the friends we had missed so much as we tried to begin a new life in South Africa.

Overwhelmed by these conflicting feelings, I broke down into fresh tears as we descended through the smog into Istanbul. Despite everything that had happened, it felt like coming home.

In the airport terminal, I delightedly listened to the melodic hum of the Turkish language, which was so familiar to me, as Petro and I navigated our way through to the immigrations counter. We were tired and anxious, but feeling confident about getting out to meet our friends in the arrivals hall as quickly as possible.

Petro was ahead of me in the line and when the immigrations officer motioned for her, she stepped up to the counter and handed over her passport. A moment later the official shook his head and asked her to step aside.

Confused, Petro protested in Turkish, "You didn't even look at my visa!"

I hurried over to the counter to join my wife. I slid my own passport across to the official and pointed to the new visa sticker issued only two days before.

"No," the official repeated. "Please wait over there."

I knew by now how these things worked; I certainly would

not just meekly stand aside and wait to see what happened. Like any good Turkish man, I noisily demanded to know what the problem was. "Can't you see we have perfectly acceptable visas? I insist you let us through! What is your problem?"

I must grant the official some respect; his ability to remain resolutely quiet in the face of such an outburst was quite impressive.

Eventually, another, apparently more important, official made her way over to us.

"Sir, Madam," she said politely. "I'm going to have to ask you to follow me. Your flight has already boarded, and is waiting for you."

"Our flight?" Petro exclaimed.

"We don't want to be on a flight. We want to be in Turkey," I argued.

She shrugged. "I'm sorry, but I cannot allow you to do that." She accepted our passports from the other officer, waved them at us, and began to walk back towards the boarding gates. "Follow me, please," she called over her shoulder.

We didn't really have much choice but to do that. Completely shocked, we trailed along behind her, trying to figure out what to do about the situation. With every step, we walked further away from the place where we wanted to be, in Turkey with our church family. To have been so close, to actually be on Turkish soil and then to be turned away at the last moment, seemed unendingly cruel. What was God up to?

Holding hands, Petro and I were speechless and unable to do much more than look at each other in confusion. Every so often, the official would ease her brisk pace and urge us to hurry. Despite our bewilderment, my wife and I took real pleasure at those moments in dawdling along even more slowly.

Eventually, despite our best efforts, we made it back to

the plane, the same one from which we had just disembarked after many hours in the air. Our passports were handed to the captain, who assessed us sternly from beneath the peak of his cap, and then we were escorted to two cordoned-off seats at the back of the plane. I felt like a naughty child being told to sit in the time-out chair.

Then we were in the air again. The big aircraft gained altitude, flying in lazy circles above Istanbul, and then set off on a straight course to Athens. From my seat, I watched in tears as the Turkish landscape disappeared from view and we were surrounded by thick, white clouds.

Though I am sure the flight attendants were not nearly convinced of my worthiness to receive their service, I asked for copies of a few of the local Turkish newspapers and pored over them during our short leg to Greece. My friends' faces stared up at me from the front pages and reminded me of happier times. The terrible incident had caused a media furor; there was page upon page of reports and editorials about what had happened.

The media had never been kind to me during my time in Turkey. I often had to withstand the worst of their scathing allegations and baseless claims. Yet now they reported with a kind of gentle repentance I did not expect. They used words like "tragedy", "disaster" and "senseless murder" to describe what had happened. They defended the very people whom they had previously sought to defame. It almost seemed as though they recognized the very real part that they had played in the build-up to the murders.

In Athens, we were forced to wait on board the plane until everyone else had disembarked and then a pair of vicious-looking Greek police officers met us at our seats. Becoming used to the whole débâcle by this stage, we stiffly left our seats to follow them and were ushered into a large, stuffy, windowless room in the bowels of the airport. With no luggage, no food and not even an explanation of what was going on, Petro and I sat down on a long metal bench in resignation. We tried to smile tiredly at the dozens of other people crammed into the room.

It was a long afternoon. For more than twelve hours we waited, unsure of what to do. I tried calling the South African embassy on my mobile phone, but as it was a public holiday, there was nobody in the office to help us. The Greek officials who made their way into the room often seemed just as frustrated about the situation as we were and seemed to be put out by what the Turks had foisted upon them. They were unable to communicate much more to us in broken English than the fact that we needed to stay put.

We knew what the outcome would be, though. We would be flown back to South Africa, our plans to return to Turkey thwarted at the very last minute. We would miss the funeral of our friend and be unable to comfort our church family. It seemed the cruelest turn of events that the Lord would allow us to get so close and then turn us away. Why would He tempt us with the possibility of success if He had not planned to complete what He had started?

Late in the evening, we were summoned again. No explanations, no apologies; only a quick walk through the international terminal, a cross-looking captain being given our passports and a humiliating march down the aisle of the plane to the very rear seats.

I now understand why you cannot book these seats in advance; they are reserved for religious extremists, such as my wife and me.

Chapter 10

$\mathcal{I}$t was a crisp autumn morning in April 2007, and the OM training base in Pretoria was shrouded in a thick, wet mist. In the small hall that served as a lecture theater, nearly 100 missionaries and trainees had gathered to share with my family and me in a memorial service for our murdered friends.

With deep reverence and passion, the young people around me sang with enthusiasm about the God who not only gives, but also takes away. They sang of surrendering all to Jesus and I wondered if many of them truly understood just what it meant to submit themselves to the mighty hand of a sovereign God.

As the time of worship drew to a close, I slowly made my way up to the lectern and surveyed the crowd. I was moved that so many would take the time to come and share in this special occasion. Haltingly, I began to speak of my dear friends. I talked about their commitment to God and their love of the Turkish people. I spoke of my pain in losing such close friends and my deep disappointment that I had been unable to go and share my grief with their family and friends in Turkey. This occasion was the closest I was going to get to an opportunity for real closure and I thanked those who had joined us for sparing the time to mourn with us.

In a solemn procession, we left the hall and walked out into the cold to a small clearing under a grove of pine trees. There, in the rocky clay soil, was a hole.

I reached for the three pictures of my friends that I had specially enlarged for this occasion.

It was not for some time after our failed attempt to get back into Turkey that I began to feel real peace about what had happened. God had known that, for some reason, it would not be good for Petro and me to be there. Perhaps it would have been too dangerous for us, or it would have distracted people there from the significance of what had happened. However, He also knew that it was important to both the Christians in Turkey and my family to know that we had at least tried. We had made every human effort possible to be there for the church in that dark hour and they knew it. Later many Turkish believers sent us messages in which they informed us that they had been blessed by knowing that, despite the risk and cost to ourselves, we had wanted to be with them.

Even if, on some level, I had begun to understand God's motives in letting us get so close, only to let us turn round again, I still felt the need to say a proper goodbye to my friends. Therefore, with the circle of OM missionaries now watching, my family and I reverently placed the photographs into the hole.

"They knew this could happen," I explained to the crowd of quiet onlookers. "They chose this life. They were not forced to sacrifice themselves, but did it willingly, out of love for Jesus and for the Turkish people."

I thought again of Tilmann, and the way his strong legs would churn at the pedals of his bicycle, ferrying him with determination to the crest of a hilltop. I saw again his face glistening with perspiration, his eyes reflecting the joy he experienced in bringing his body into submission and forcing it to accomplish the task he had assigned to it.

"I cannot imagine what those last moments were like for them," I said solemnly. "I know they suffered. However, I also know that they would have remained faithful to the end. I have no doubt that they gave up their lives willingly and bravely.

"I am also sure that God gave them the strength to accept the path that He had chosen for them. They entered eternity as His obedient children receiving praise from the Father. Though the process was extremely harsh, I know with certainty that on that day they were born into a very real and much more wonderful, eternal life."

Martin Junior and Benjamin stepped forward to plant a small wooden cross at the foot of the makeshift grave from which the faces of Uğur, Necati and Tilmann smiled up at us. Then, with a child's enthusiasm, Samuel pinned their names to the arms of the cross.

"We leave this cross as a testimony of their sacrifice," I said. "When we see it, may we also be reminded to consider if we would be willing to pay the ultimate price for our Savior."

There were some nods in the crowd. Some of these students were themselves preparing to head out in missionary service to other far-flung, dangerous parts of the world: the Middle East, unreached Asia and Muslim Africa. Surely they had also asked themselves if they would be willing to give up their lives.

"It may not be the last cross we need to place here," I added.

There, in that rocky soil, we buried the photographs and then quietly filed away. In the tawny winter grasslands only the simple wooden cross remained visible, a lasting symbol of remembrance for all who saw it.

I wondered, though, why my name wasn't on the cross as well.

This became perhaps the biggest unresolved issue in my heart in the months following the killings in Malatya. I wondered not so much why my friends had to die; that, to me, was clear. We all understood the dangers of living and working as missionaries in Muslim Turkey, as well as the promises from Jesus that we were to expect persecution and even death for His name's sake. In some ways, we all understood that it had only been a matter of time before someone in our team in Turkey would have been asked to pay the ultimate price for their faith.

Yet, as the leader of the team and the very person who had led each of the three individuals into the ministry in Malatya, I felt extreme guilt and even a little bit cheated. Should not the price have been mine to pay? Why had God removed me from the scene just a few short months earlier, rather than allow me to give up my life with my friends? I did not have some kind of perverse desire to die, but certainly would have considered it an honor to have been deemed worthy to make that kind of sacrifice.

In prayer, I wrestled with God over this issue. Why had the leader been spared and the followers taken? While the grief diminished over time and the guilt became more bearable, the question remained.

It was only several years later that I felt this concern had been truly dealt with. In 2011, I was privileged to meet an OM missionary named Gary Witherall for the second time. Gary and his wife Bonnie had been workers for OM in the south of Lebanon. They enjoyed a vibrant young marriage, a successfully growing ministry, and a real love of the life they had in the balmy Mediterranean city in which they lived.

Then, in 2004, Gary had received a terrifying phone call. He raced to the women's clinic where his wife worked, only to discover her lifeless body in a pool of blood. She had been shot in the head, at point-blank range, by Muslim extremists.

Prevented by police from getting any closer to his wife's body, he had lain on the floor in an adjoining room, all but overcome by grief, but still capable of realizing that in that moment God was offering him a choice – to hate, or to forgive. He chose the latter.

When I told Gary about the guilt I still carried with me and the problems I had understanding why God had spared me yet accepted the sacrifice of my friends, his answer was simple: "Someone had to be left behind to tell the story. If you had died with them, perhaps a very important message to the church would have died as well. Maybe God spared you simply as a means of ensuring that the message He wanted to convey through their deaths lives on."

This, then, has become the purpose of my life. In the five years since the tragedy in Malatya, I have been privileged to share the story of my three friends with thousands of people across South Africa and the world. As missionaries who have lived through some of the realities of service in a foreign country, we have been welcomed with open arms to share our experiences in hundreds of churches. My message to them is clear: look beyond yourselves and realize the calling that God has placed on the church. We have become a generation consumed with ourselves. The ways in which we spend our money, manage our time and reveal our public identity on Facebook all testify to this. Yet I am convinced that God wants us to raise our eyes to the horizon, and look beyond our own needs to those of the multitudes who have never before heard of or received the love of Jesus.

Petro and I cannot return to Turkey – certainly not for lack of trying – but what we can do is mobilize people in our place to take the gospel to the very ends of the earth.

In John chapter 20, Jesus appears to His disciples after His miraculous resurrection. First, He tells them, "Peace be with you." Then, boldly, He proclaims: "As the Father has sent me, I am sending you." Yet we, as a body, seem to have lost sight of this serious instruction. We have become more concerned with the state of our church building fund than the state of the world. We console ourselves for our lack of action by worrying and being without faith: "Where would we get the money? How would our family react? What would happen to our children's education?" While these are legitimate concerns, we should not allow them to keep us from being obedient and stepping out in faith.

I believe Jesus spoke the truth when He said, "But seek his kingdom and his righteousness, and all these things will be given to you as well" (Matthew 6:33). I believe this not just because I believe in the inerrancy of Scripture, but also because I have seen God come through for my family and me. When faced with struggles during our years in ministry, we were never abandoned by God. The tough times were real and difficult while they lasted; yet God was always there to help and encourage us.

Even death ceases to be such a terrifying prospect when you are certain of your place in the will of God.

Tertullian, the early Christian theologian, wrote: "The blood of the martyrs is the seed of the church." This has certainly been the case in Malatya. In the years since the killings, the church in Malatya has only grown. Many new members have joined, perhaps in part encouraged by the sacrifice of love shown for them by Necati, Tilmann and Uğur. There is even a thriving deaf contingent of the local congregation, with all church services offered not only in Turkish, but also in sign language to accommodate their needs. The importance of missionary work is part of the Malatya congregation's core DNA. Despite the fact that they themselves are still on the receiving end of support from international missionaries, the Christians in that church also financially support needy congregations and foreign workers in other nations.

Even the city council of Malatya has changed in the last few years. I remember when we first arrived there the cold indifference of the people toward the gospel, the fear of foreigners and the historic reputation of the place as a town in which Christians were killed. Now, the city council that refused to allow Tilmann's body to be buried in the local graveyard is paying for the old, decaying Armenian church building to be restored and to be opened again as a center for Christian worship. It stood, condemned and rotting, silently testifying to its emptiness, for many years. Now it will be filled with people again and offer a place for seekers to come and learn about the resurrected Savior of the world.

In downtown Malatya, Tilmann's grave still stands as a lasting sign of the sacrifices made to bring God's message of truth to that city. It is not a symbol of defeat, but of victory, because for believers, who have hope in Jesus, to die is gain.

Also serving as a testimony to God's grace in that city are the foreign missionaries, who either stayed behind despite the dangers to which they and their families were exposed, or have returned in the years since then. Susanne is still in Malatya with her children, an irrefutable beacon of God's love to the local people, as well as His ability to forgive. With her are many new workers, who have heeded God's call and forsaken other opportunities back home in order to preach the gospel in a foreign place, which has proved to be a dangerous one.

As for my family and me, I sometimes wonder whether we are still living on the edge of Paradise. Certainly, our geographic location is no longer in that amazing historical region, with its ragged-edged mountain ranges, rich, fertile valleys and broad rivers. The season for us to be in Turkey, perhaps the historical Eden, is over.

Yet today we live with an intense awareness of the transient nature of our lives. We might be called on to give up our lives, or even lose them unexpectedly and so be ushered into a new life in eternity, at any moment. The fence between this life and the next, as I have seen through the lives and deaths of my friends, is very fragile indeed. God's timing is perfect and in the blink of an eye we may be removed from our lives here and finally be transported into the fullness of His presence there.

This is no less true for any believer, although Petro, my boys and I are privileged in having had our spirits truly awakened to this fact. Our lives will extend beyond the physical experiences we encounter here on earth. The few years which God grants us in this troubled world are just an insignificant dot on the whole timeline of eternity, which we will experience in His presence. We understand from the Bible that the choices we make in these few, short years will have a direct bearing on our satisfaction in heaven. However, all too often, our focus is on hoarding happiness and comfort here and now, instead of making an imperishable investment there.

I have stood at the brink of Paradise. On a number of occasions, I have closely faced the prospect of meeting face to face with my Savior. This is a prospect as exhilarating as it is terrifying. Will He be pleased with the way in which I have modeled my life after Him? Will He greet me with the reward of "Well done, good and faithful servant"? Or will I, as one escaping through fire, slink red-faced into His awesome presence?

I still live on the edge of Paradise, although it is sometimes less obvious than during the years I spent in Turkey. I still don't know when the sun will set on my time here and a new day will dawn in eternity for me with an all-illuminating brightness. In the meantime, I choose to live each day with the abandon, fearlessness and love for my God that Jesus taught me through my missionary experiences.

Together, He and I will live on the edge of Paradise.

Epilogue

fter nearly four years, the trial of the men accused of murdering Tilmann, Uğur and Necati has not yet been concluded. They have remained in custody this entire time, while court proceedings continue to drag on.

As more and more details of the crime come to light, a greater conspiracy has been exposed, which has come to be known as the Eregenkom Conspiracy. Its aim was to try to destabilize the Turkish government, in part by forcing out Christians and discrediting missionary groups within the country. The trials of government officials involved in this plot have been joined to the Malatya hearing.

Meanwhile, the church in Turkey continues to grow, albeit slowly. More Turks are coming forward to join the ranks of believers as outspoken followers of Jesus Christ the Messiah. The many years of faithful labor by missionaries to Turkey were not in vain. Jesus will build His church, and nothing will be able to destroy it.

Our hearts are still beating strong for the nation of Turkey and her people. It is our dream that Turks right across the world will come to know Jesus and His love in a very personal way.

One day, my telephone rang. It was Jan, the director of OM in France. He asked me if I knew that there were more than half a million Turks in France, and virtually no one to share the love of Jesus with them in their native language. Jan then asked us if we would consider moving to Paris and starting with a church planting project amongst the Turks…

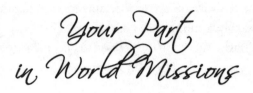

Your Part in World Missions

Operation Mobilisation is an international mission organization with ministries in over 110 nations of the world. Founded in 1957, the ministry has grown from a handful of students to more than 6,000 full-time workers from all over the world.

You may be asking where you, as a Christian, fit into God's plan for the salvation of the world. Here are a few ways in which you can become involved right now!

- *You can pray.* Become informed about God's world. Ask for information about missionaries in areas of particular interest to you. Stand before God on behalf of your brothers and sisters on the mission field. Pray for more missionaries to be called and sent to reach the lost for Christ. Don't be surprised if God uses you to answer your own prayers!

- *You can give.* God has given you the privilege of being responsible for a portion of His money. Decide how much you may keep for yourself, then use the rest to further God's kingdom. One way is to support foreign mission work.

- *You can send.* Look around in your church or community. Seek out another who senses a call to become a missionary, then spur them on and encourage them to further seek God's direction for their life. Adopt missionaries. Give them moral support. Encourage them through letters, tapes or emails; let them know that you believe in them and in the work God has called them to do. Maybe you are in the position to offer them a place to stay or a car to use while they're on home assignments.

- *You can go.* The Great Commission is a call to you too! You can see the need. Why delay?

Contact us if you want to know more: www.om.org

OM USA
PO Box 444 Tyrone, GA 30290. Tel: +1 770 631 0432.

OM UK
The Quinta, Weston Rhyn, Oswestry, Shropshire SY10 7LT. Tel: +44 (0)1691 773388.

OM Australia
PO Box 32, Box Hill, VIC 3128. Tel: +61 (0)3 9898 9348.

OM New Zealand
PO Box 76882, Manukau 2241. Tel: +64 (0)9 298 0802.

OM Netherlands
Assemblageweg 9, 8304 BB Emmeloord. Tel: +31 0527 615607.

OM Canada

84 West Street, Port Colborne, ON L3K 4C8. Tel: +1 905 835 2546.

OM Ships

Alte Neckarelzer Str. 2, 74821 Mosbach, Germany. Tel: +49 (0)6261 92630.

OM South Africa

Private Bag X03, Lynnwood Ridge 0040, Pretoria. Tel: +27 (0)12 807 0162.